Palgrave Studies in International Relations Se

General Editors:

Knud Erik Jørgensen, Department of Political Science, University of Aarhus, Denmark

Audie Klotz, Department of Political Science, Maxwell School of Citizenship and Public Affairs, Syracuse University, USA

Palgrave Studies in International Relations, produced in association with the ECPR Standing Group for International Relations, will provide students and scholars with the best theoretically-informed scholarship on the global issues of our time. Edited by Knud Erik Jørgensen and Audie Klotz, this new book series will comprise cutting-edge monographs and edited collections which bridge schools of thought and cross the boundaries of conventional fields of study.

Titles include:

Pami Aalto, Vilho Harle and Sami Moisio (*editors*)
INTERNATIONAL STUDIES
Interdisciplinary Approaches

Mathias Albert, Lars-Erik Cederman and Alexander Wendt (*editors*)
NEW SYSTEMS THEORIES OF WORLD POLITICS

Barry Buzan and Ana Gonzalez-Pelaez (*editors*)
INTERNATIONAL SOCIETY AND THE MIDDLE EAST
English School Theory at the Regional Level

Toni Erskine and Richard Ned Lebow (*editors*)
TRAGEDY IN INTERNATIONAL RELATIONS

Geir Hønneland
BORDERLAND RUSSIANS
Identity, Narrative and International Relations

Oliver Kessler, Rodney Bruce Hall, Cecelia Lynch and Nicholas G. Onuf (*editors*)
ON RULES, POLITICS AND KNOWLEDGE
Friedrich Kratochwil, International Relations, and Domestic Affairs

Pierre P. Lizee
A WHOLE NEW WORLD
Reinventing International Studies for the Post-Western World

Hans J. Morgenthau, Hartmut Behr and Felix Rösch
THE CONCEPT OF THE POLITICAL

Cornelia Navari (*editor*)
THEORISING INTERNATIONAL SOCIETY
English School Methods

Dirk Peters
CONSTRAINED BALANCING: THE EU'S SECURITY POLICY

Simon F. Reich
GLOBAL NORMS, AMERICAN SPONSORSHIP AND THE EMERGING
PATTERNS OF WORLD POLITICS

Robbie Shilliam
GERMAN THOUGHT AND INTERNATIONAL RELATIONS
The Rise and Fall of a Liberal Project

Daniela Tepe
THE MYTH ABOUT GLOBAL CIVIL SOCIETY
Domestic Politics to Ban Landmines

Daniel C. Thomas (*editor*)
MAKING EU FOREIGN POLICY
National Preferences, European Norms and Common Policies

Rens van Munster
SECURITIZING IMMIGRATION
The Politics of Risk in the EU

Palgrave Studies In International Relations Series
Series Standing Order ISBN 978–0–230–20063–0 (hardback)
978–0–230–24115–2 (paperback)

You can receive future titles in this series as they are published by placing a standing order. Please contact your bookseller or, in case of difficulty, write to us at the address below with your name and address, the title of the series and one of the ISBNs quoted above.

Customer Services Department, Macmillan Distribution Ltd, Houndmills, Basingstoke, Hampshire RG21 6XS, England

The Concept of the Political

Hans J. Morgenthau

Edited by

Hartmut Behr

and

Felix Rösch

Translated by

Maeva Vidal

First published 2012 by
PALGRAVE MACMILLAN

Palgrave Macmillan in the UK is an imprint of Macmillan Publishers Limited,
registered in England, company number 785998, of Houndmills, Basingstoke,
Hampshire RG21 6XS.

Palgrave Macmillan in the US is a division of St Martin's Press LLC,
175 Fifth Avenue, New York, NY 10010.

Palgrave Macmillan is the global academic imprint of the above companies
and has companies and representatives throughout the world.

Palgrave® and Macmillan® are registered trademarks in the United States,
the United Kingdom, Europe and other countries

ISBN: 978–0–230–36308–3 hardback
ISBN: 978–0–230–36309–0 paperback

This book is printed on paper suitable for recycling and made from fully
managed and sustained forest sources. Logging, pulping and manufacturing
processes are expected to conform to the environmental regulations of the
country of origin.

A catalogue record for this book is available from the British Library.

A catalog record for this book is available from the Library of Congress.

10 9 8 7 6 5 4 3 2 1
21 20 19 18 17 16 15 14 13 12

Printed and bound in Great Britain by
CPI Antony Rowe, Chippenham and Eastbourne

Contents

Acknowledgments   vii

Foreword   ix
Michael C. Williams

Part I   Introduction
Hartmut Behr and Felix Rösch

1   Overview of Morgenthau's Oeuvre and Worldview   3

2   Contextualization of "The Concept of the Political"   15

3   Morgenthau's Epistemological Commitments   33

4   Morgenthau's Twofold Concept of Power   47

Part II   The Concept of the Political and the Theory of International Disputes
Hans J. Morgenthau

Translator's Note
Maeva Vidal   83

Preface   85

1   Introduction   86

2   On the Concept of Legal Disputes   88

3   The Concept of the Political   96

4   On the Concept of Political Disputes   121

5   Conclusion   134

*Annex 1   Bibliography of Hans J. Morgenthau
(Published and Unpublished Academic Work in
Chronological Order)*   146

Annex 2   Biography of Hans J. Morgenthau,
Including the Publication Years of His Major Monographs   154

Name Index   159

Subject Index   161

Acknowledgments

This edition, like any academic work, would not have been possible without the help of many colleagues and friends, as well as understanding and supportive family members. Instead of producing and presenting a list of these through enumeration, we took the liberty of mentioning those most significant, academically speaking, in their relation to this project and do apologize at the same time for having (certainly) forgotten someone. Although this most often appears at the end of acknowledgments, we feel we should rather mention at the beginning that the editors are responsible for any errors that may appear in this tome. This edition most challengingly involved much meticulous research into another author's annotations and footnotes; the systematization and interpretation of archival material, including letters, slips and paper clippings, postcards, handwritten notes and so on; and the translation of a complex linguistic mélange resulting from a native German speaker (i.e., Hans J. Morgenthau), educated and writing in the 1930s still in the sometimes convoluted language of German *Staatsrechtslehre*, writing this monograph in French as a second language, being here and now translated into English some 80 years later. The potential for mistakes, distortions, limitations of translatability and the like is evidently enormous, and since we undertook this project responsibility for any errors is exclusively ours.

The initial idea for this project, studying Hans J. Morgenthau's early works and preparing an English translation of *La notion du "politique"*, emerged in a discussion with Michael Williams a few years ago in 2006. It is therefore only appropriate – and we are very grateful – that Michael has written the Foreword for this edition and given us many helpful comments on the translation and introduction. Since the mention of colleagues and friends in this acknowledgment does not reflect the relevance of support and advice but rather the genealogy of how this project developed, we are next grateful to Susanna and Matthew Morgenthau, Hans J. Morgenthau's daughter and son and holders of the copyright of their father's work, as their granting us the copyright for *La notion du "politique"* was, of course, a most crucial condition for this edition to be made possible. We wish to thank them both deeply for their support of this project, for their advice and for their cooperation. Also, the thoughtful care and attention with which they discussed and dealt with their father's work and legacy were impressive and very instructive. Next in the genealogy is Maeva Vidal from Ottawa, who provided an excellent translation of Morgenthau's book, putting great effort and consideration into questions of translation and translatability of individual terminologies and sentences. In this context we are grateful to the research committee of the Faculty of Humanities and Social Sciences at Newcastle University for their provision of a translation grant. With particular regard to the production of the translation we also want to express our deep thanks to Christoph Frei for his review of the translation and his many helpful suggestions, especially regarding legal terminologies.

Next in the genealogy of this project – increasingly devoted as the project approached finalization – is Christina M. Brian and her team at Palgrave Macmillan. It was great to experience this kind of professional, passionate, and reliable cooperation; many thanks – we are looking forward to future projects. Concerning the publication of this edition, we would also like to thank Knud Erik Jørgensen and Audie Klotz as the editors of Palgrave Macmillan's *Studies in International Relations* for their recruitment of this book into the series. Much material used here for the introduction and the translation is from the Morgenthau archive at the Law Library, Library of Congress, Washington DC. We wish to thank the archive staff for their very helpful role in accessing the material and sifting through some 200 boxes of paper slips, photocopies, letters and so on. Last, but not least, our deep thanks go to the panelists and attendants – primarily Seán Molloy, Michael Williams, Vibeke Schou Tjalve, and Oliver Jütersonke – of our workshop on Morgenthau's concept of the political at the Annual Convention of the British International Studies Association (BISA) held at Manchester in April 2011 for their discussions and for sharing important knowledge and material on Morgenthau.

Hartmut Behr and Felix Rösch
Newcastle upon Tyne, UK

Foreword

The recent resurgence of interest in the political thought of Hans J. Morgenthau has been striking. After decades of neglect or near caricature by both his supporters and his critics, Morgenthau has once again emerged as a serious figure within international political theory. At one level, this revival clearly has its roots in political events, particularly the ways that the "muscular Wilsonianism" of American foreign policy in the early years of the new millennium made political realism seem to many an attractive intellectual inspiration, a powerful rhetorical resource, and even a compelling political alternative. Yet the interest in Morgenthau and realism more broadly clearly goes well beyond the response to a particular set of political circumstances, and it should in no way be identified narrowly with the advocacy of a return to power politics, or even with a general injunction toward restraint and prudence in foreign policy. For this interest also reflects a deeper desire to explore the ways that a broader appreciation of "classical" realism can be used to reconnect the field of International Relations to wider traditions of political thought from which it has often become estranged, and to examine its relationship to contemporary developments in International Relations theory. In these forms, the nuanced and sophisticated visions of Morgenthau and realism that have appeared of late are part of a broad and ambitious agenda that seeks in various ways to revivify international political theory by reopening the stale and often sterile narratives about its evolution, and by bringing past and present thinking and traditional and critical theorizing into a fruitful dialogue.

This translation of *La notion du "politique" et la théorie des différends internationaux* is in this context both timely and significant. While this text, with its overt focus on legal debates of the early twentieth century, may sometimes seem far distant from many versions of realism and much of International Relations theory today, it in fact expresses concerns that are central to political realism. At the heart of these concerns, as the title indicates, is the complex and controversial "concept of the political" itself – a concept whose correct understanding Morgenthau, like many others before him, considered essential for any cogent theory of political life. Indeed, Morgenthau's rendering of this key concept was, as he clearly understood, at the heart of his vision of politics. It provided not only the basis for the assessment of the potential and limitations of international law that was at the heart of his emerging theory of political realism: it was also crucial in differentiating his theory of power politics both from traditional understandings of *realpolitik* and from contending political visions on the Left and the Right that also claimed to find their foundation in a particular understanding of "the political". For all their apparent abstraction, the issues at stake in this conceptual question were crucial – and they had direct implications for domestic as well as international politics, and for the connection between the two.

There is little doubt that Morgenthau's thinking underwent significant evolution in the years following the publication of *La notion du "politique"*. International law came to play a less and less central role in his writings. But there is equally little doubt that the concern with fundamental questions of political life addressed in this text and expressed in legal terms remained important parts of his political vision, and that they comprised key – if often implicit (and sometimes even hidden) – elements of his theory of international politics. Indeed, any cogent appreciation of realism as a set of philosophical and political claims, as a "tradition" of thought, as well as of Morgenthau's particular version of it, needs to include a consideration of the core conceptual questions that Morgenthau takes up in these brief chapters. As such, their translation and republication, along with the extensive intellectual and historical contextualization produced by the editors, provides a significant resource not only for disciplinary historians, but also for anyone interested in the nature of political realism and its vision of world politics.

Michael C. Williams

Part I
Introduction

Hartmut Behr and Felix Rösch

1
Overview of Morgenthau's Oeuvre and Worldview

The German-American political scientist Hans J. Morgenthau (1904–1980) is widely considered to be the doyen of International Relations (Hoffmann, 1977, p. 44; Kissinger, 1980, p. 14; Fromkin, 1993, p. 81; Kindermann, 2004, p. 85). Due to the enormous success of his textbook *Politics Among Nations*, which was first published in 1948, and to being considered to be one of the leading figures of the realist school of thought, Morgenthau's name was already in his lifetime added to the canon of International Relations and his thought is now of recurrent concern in the sociology of knowledge of the discipline of International Relations and in international political theory. *Politics Among Nations* eventually became the most widely used textbook in International Relations curricula in higher education institutions in the United States and is now in its ninth edition.

Despite the undisputed importance of Morgenthau for the development of International Relations as an academic discipline, he eventually became marginalized and his thought suffered intellectual damage due to widespread misinterpretations. The reasons do not have to concern us here, not least because they were elaborated elsewhere (Bain, 2000; Behr, 2005; Behr and Heath, 2009), but, still, we have to remark that Morgenthau was, although often cited, hardly ever read (Williams, 2005, p. 82). References were primarily made to the famous "Six Principles of Political Realism" which Morgenthau added to the second edition of *Politics Among Nations*, after colleagues, whose verdict Morgenthau considered highly, suggested that it be adapted more with the requirements of a textbook in mind (HJM-Archive Box 121). Apart from *Politics Among Nations*, Morgenthau's oeuvre attracted little interest among scholars of International

Relations. Particularly neglected were Morgenthau's writings investigating his ontological and epistemological framework, such as his first American monograph *Scientific Man vs Power Politics* (1946) or *Science: Servant or Master?* (1972). Equally, anthologies which covered all aspects of his worldview, such as the three volumes of *Politics in the Twentieth Century* (1962) or *Truth and Power* (1970), were hardly ever consulted to assess Morgenthau's contribution to the study of international politics. Even less interest was given to Morgenthau's European writings. Only recently did scholarship develop an interest in these works in the context of scholarly concern with the intellectual history of the discipline (Frei, 2001; Tjalve, 2008; Scheuerman, 2009; Jütersonke, 2010).

The present translation of Morgenthau's study *The Concept of the Political* (*La notion du "politique" et la théorie des différends internationaux*) from 1933 is, therefore, the first endeavor to make his European writings more accessible to students of International Relations, particularly of the English-speaking academia, by presenting a translation of his original French text. *The Concept of the Political* seems at first not well suited for this undertaking since it is a little-known, rather short study Morgenthau published between his doctoral thesis *Die internationale Rechtspflege, ihr Wesen und ihre Grenzen* (*International Judicature, Its Nature and Limits*[1]) from 1929 and his Habilitation (post-doctoral degree) *La Réalité des normes. En particulier des normes du droit international. Fondement d'une théorie des normes* (*The Reality of Norms in International Law: On the Foundations of a Theory or Norms*) from 1934. Even those scholars who cite European works of Morgenthau do not usually refer to this study. Still, *The Concept of the Political* was chosen because, unlike his jurisprudential writings, this study was Morgenthau's first political elaboration and marks his transition from jurisprudence toward political science. It is, furthermore, *fundamental* for students of Morgenthau's thought and of international politics because it is his most extensive elaboration of the concept of the political as the central factor of any human sociation and the study of politics.

To avoid further misinterpretations of Morgenthau's work and to introduce his writing *The Concept of the Political*, the following introduction will provide, first, an overview of the development of Morgenthau's worldview and will contextualize this writing within it. We will then provide a contextualization of this work in the legal and political debates of his time as well as in the current debates of International Relations. In a third step we will introduce more specifically the major ontological and epistemological aspects of Morgenthau's political theory before, in a final step, elaborating his twofold concept of power, consisting of an empirical and a normative notion.

The particular insight offered by a translation of *The Concept of the Political* lies in the fact that Morgenthau's worldview rested fundamentally on the personal and intellectual experiences he had as a young scholar in Germany, Switzerland, and Spain during the latter half of the 1920s and the early 30s. Certainly, later on Morgenthau had experiences that led to alterations and amendments of his thoughts like the US wars in Korea and Vietnam, nuclear armament and his assessment of the United Nations or the European Coal and Steel Community. Nevertheless, there were no fundamental changes to his worldview with regard to ontological and epistemological commitments during his lifetime. In the 1950s, Morgenthau was still under the impression left by the downfall of the League of Nations and the final collapse of the Weimar Republic which he had experienced while in Geneva in the 1930s. Therefore, he was skeptical about the promises of international institutions and mass democracy. In the 1960s, however, Morgenthau's opinion of the United Nations changed since he realized that it would offer, despite its organizational shortcomings, an international forum in which divergent national politics could be negotiated and a viable compromise eventually reached. Similarly, the development of weapons of mass destruction led Morgenthau to an even firmer belief that the nation-state as a form of human sociation would become outdated, due to its destructive power, and would have to be replaced by a world community (Morgenthau, 1952b, p. 131; 1954, pp. 81–2; 1962a, pp. 75–6). None of these experiences, however, were fundamental enough to completely alter his worldview and Morgenthau's political thought remained within the cosmos of continental European humanities and social sciences. This is evidenced in the Preface to *Science: Servant or Master?* in which he acknowledged that part of this last monograph was based on his unpublished manuscript "Über den Sinn der Wissenschaft in dieser Zeit und über die Bestimmung des Menschen" ("On the Meaning of Humanities and the Nature of Men") from 1934 (Morgenthau, 1934b, p. XXI).

Morgenthau, the son of a liberal Jewish physician from the then Ernestine town of Cobourg in southern Germany, studied law at the University of Munich, but also attended lectures by the historian Hermann Oncken and the art historian Heinrich Wölfflin (Morgenthau, 1984, p. 5). In 1928 he transferred to the University of Frankfurt to finish his doctoral thesis. In Frankfurt, Morgenthau also worked as a clerk at the chambers of the well-known labor lawyer Hugo Sinzheimer which allowed him to experience an unprecedented intellectual atmosphere. Morgenthau not only got to know various members of the Institute for Social Research, such as Theodor W. Adorno, Max Horkheimer, Herbert Marcuse, and Erich Fromm, but also Karl Mannheim whose office was in the same building as his own at the time (Frei, 2001, pp. 38–9; Postscript, 1984, pp. 348–9; Lebow, 2003, p. 253); among his colleagues were also leading intellectuals like Ernst Fraenkel and Franz Neumann who became prominent representatives of post-Second World War political science. In this intellectual environment Morgenthau developed three concepts that remained the fundaments of his worldview: the disenchantment of the world; pariah; and the power of dissent.

The disenchantment of the world

With the disenchantment of the world, to use a term by Max Weber (2004, p. 30), Morgenthau's anti-ideological stance is emphasized (Molloy, 2004, p. 8). The cultural crisis of the Weimar Republic fostered the development of ideologies. Life in its totality went out of joint due to dramatic changes and, consequently, seemed incomprehensible. Ideologies had filled a metaphysical void, forming "political religions" (Eric Voegelin). They seemed able to serve the needs of the masses providing shelter from their yearning for the meaning of life. Although Morgenthau at times argued the need to acknowledge the urgency of re-establishing a metaphysical system (Morgenthau, 1937, pp. 8–11) because it would enable humans to find a meaning in life again (Morgenthau, 1930a, p. 42), he still remained critical toward the promises of ideologies. A metaphysical system would have to guarantee empirical and normative objectivity[2] (Morgenthau, 1937, pp. 97–100); ideologies, however, would not be able to provide that kind of objectivity because they would remain subject to their particular time and culture, despite their obscuring of their own perspectivist outlook. Mannheim had identified hitherto mainly four types of ideologies in his study on *Ideology and Utopia* (originally published in 1929) which dominated the political discourse at that time as well as Morgenthau's world-view: socialism, conservatism, liberalism, and fascism (Mannheim, 1984, pp. 117–46).

As noted, in 1936 Morgenthau worked in Frankfurt for Sinzheimer who brought him into contact with members of the Frankfurt School. In addition, representatives of conservatism also affected Morgenthau. They promoted a conservative revolution by arguing the importance of recreating a worthwhile cultural and political sys-tem which had evaporated with the collapse of the German Empire after the First World War and were in agreement in their denial of the Weimar Republic, which they regarded as a weak state without real sovereignty. Morgenthau came into contact with this kind of thought in the work of Carl Schmitt whom he had studied, like his colleagues from Sinzheimer's law office, in his quest to develop an approach capable of properly reflecting reality within the field of *Staatslehre* (Scheuerman, 2009, p. 32). And yet, Morgenthau came to the conclusion that he was neither a Marxist nor in agreement with Schmitt, the later "*Kronjurist* of the Third Reich" (Waldemar Gurian), whom Morgenthau, after having met him personally, considered to be "the most evil man alive" (Morgenthau, 1984, p. 16) due to his complete lack of a "*geistig-seelisches Zentrum*" (spiritual-moral person-ality) (Morgenthau, 1932).

Thus, Morgenthau criticized ideologies from both sides, social-ist and conservative, for their inability to recognize the spatial and temporal contingencies and conditionalities of political knowledge and political order. This inability would seduce representatives of ideologies into promoting their ideas as eternal truths and would convince them that truth could be detected by pursuing structural approaches which considered life to be historically or biologically determined and thus a teleological process. As Morgenthau pointed out on an undated slip, "[t]he idea of scientism is clearly recognizable here [Marxism], the idea that you only need to use the right formula to apply to the right mechanical device, and the political subjugation of man will disappear" (HJM-Archive Box 30). Any kind of struc-tural or positivist approach was dismissed by Morgenthau because it contradicted what he believed politics consisted of. We read in his doctoral thesis:

> We have to remark that a distinction between political and non-political questions which depends on their purposes is impossible, because the concept of the political is neither bound with conceptual necessity to a particular purpose, nor can it be excluded from any purpose ... The concept of the political does not have a fixed substance; it is rather a feature, a quality, a coloring, which can be attached to any kind of substance. (Morgenthau, 1929, p. 67; translation by the authors)

Hence, politics is based for Morgenthau on fundamental normative assumptions, expressed in diverse and antagonistic interests pursued in the interactions between people(s). These assumptions would be subject to change and thus would create different temporal and spatial conditions of politics and political knowledge. As Morgenthau put it by referring to Mannheim: "[P]olitical thinking is ... '*standortgebunden*', that is to say, it is tied to a particular situation" (Morgenthau, 1962a, pp. 72–3).

The conscious pariah

The second concept that fundamentally informed Morgenthau's worldview is, in consideration of Hannah Arendt, termed "conscious pariah" (Arendt, 1978, pp. 65–6) or alienation.

Within Morgenthau's socializing intellectual field, the two most prominent attempts to use the epistemological figure of alienation were written by Georg Simmel and Alfred Schütz. Both follow different conceptions of alienation. While Simmel focuses on the stranger within a society – that is, "the person who comes today and stays tomorrow" (Simmel, 1964, p. 402), exemplified in the history of European Jews – Schütz referred to the stranger as an outsider, manifested in the ideal type of the emigrant. Hence, the stranger was for Schütz "an adult individual ... who tries to be permanently accepted or at least tolerated by the group which he approaches" (Schütz, 1944, p. 499). Despite the difference in these definitions, both praised the particular epistemological insight which the actual experience and conceptualization of alienation would provide. This would be expected as, among other things, the stranger would be better suited to rationally analyze his/her environment, having more "freedom" (Simmel, 1964, p. 405) due to a detachment from social conditions and obligations which determine the perception and thoughts of people living immediately under these conditions and having been socialized by them all their life. Furthermore, Schütz emphasized that alienation might increase the stranger's knowledge compared to people who were well-established within their respective societies and who would not have to question their everyday actions and common beliefs, as the stranger had to do (Schütz, 1944, p. 500). Whereas for Simmel the enhanced mobility of the stranger was essential because it would enable the stranger to acquire more knowledge due to his/her more numerous experiences, Schütz also acknowledged the burden that alienation would put on the stranger which he/she had to deal with intellectually and actively. These thoughts apply to Morgenthau's worldview since he was exposed to both physical and intellectual alienation, gradually turning his life circumstances into a fundamental basis for his worldview (see also Frei, 2001, p. 23).

On the one hand, Morgenthau was a stranger in Europe in the sense of Simmel because of his family and religious background. Morgenthau grew up as the only child of an authoritarian father. Although patriarchy was then common, it left scars in Morgenthau's psyche in the form of shyness and the fear of being rejected (Postscript, 1984, pp. 339–41; Frei, 2005, p. 39). The family, however, was not the only source of Morgenthau's alienation. What made matters worse, was that Morgenthau grew up in Cobourg, where already in 1929 the Nazi Party (*Nationalsozialistische Deutsche Arbeiterpartei*, or NSDAP) had won an absolute majority in city council elections (Hayward and Morris, 1988, pp. 110–15). Life as a Jew in such an anti-Semitic area was difficult and lonely. This was evident in an incident at the Scouts: "I remember being spit at when marching in a group. This treatment aggravated the traumatic experiences I had at home and led to a kind of retrenchment. I retreated into my own shell in fear of disappointing human contacts" (Postscript, 1984, p. 339). Participation in the Scouts, just like membership in the fraternity "Thuringia" (HJM-Archive Box 44), which he joined partly because of his father's wishes, demonstrates that Morgenthau made various efforts to overcome alienation and become an unquestioned member of German society. This kind of alienation was certainly aggravated when he was forced to leave Europe and seek adoption by a new society in America (Postscript, 1984, p. 348).

As an intellectual, Morgenthau's forced emigration was, as Neumann, his former colleague in Sinzheimer's office remarked, threefold: not only was he displaced, from his friends and belongings, but he was also displaced as a scholar from his intellectual field and, finally, as a political person, who promoted republican and humane politics (Eisfeld, 1991, p. 116). Unlike other émigré scholars, however, he was also a "double exile" since he was not only expelled from Germany, but also from Spain where he had tried to settle after his fleeing as a refugee from Germany and Switzerland (HJM-Archive Box 22). Hence, Morgenthau was forced twice in his life to adapt to new life-worlds; the second time was especially difficult for Morgenthau. He knew nobody in the United States as his only acquaintance, Richard Gottheil, a professor at Columbia University, had died shortly before Morgenthau arrived in 1937 (Postscript, 1984, p. 364). This meant not only personal and social hardship, but also a worsening of his anxiety in terms of securing a position in American academia.

His first academic position at Brooklyn College required him to teach "just about everything under the sun" (Postscript, 1984, p. 367). One problem was the different intellectual tradition in the United States in which liberalism was the ruling dogma. In accordance with his anti-ideological stance, Morgenthau warned early on of the dangers an exaggerated understanding of liberalism would cause. This almost intransigent understanding of philosophical traditions is manifested in his remark to Rita Neumeyer Herbert from June 2, 1947, when he stated, after reading the reviews of his *Scientific Man vs Power Politics*, that "they [the Americans] literally don't know what I am talking about" (HJM-Archive Box 26). Indeed, shared intellectual traditions and some form of intellectual alienation might explain why most of Morgenthau's friends were European emigrants. It is to be assumed that there was a particular bond between German-speaking émigrés. Elisabeth Young-Bruehl remarked, regarding the circle around Arendt to which Morgenthau belonged, that these were people "... who could respond to a quotation from Goethe with a quotation from Heine, who knew German fairy tales" (Young-Bruehl, 1982, p. XIV).

On the one hand, Morgenthau was an immigrant; he was also a stranger in Schütz's sense. It is reasonable to believe that, early on, Morgenthau was aware of the possibilities alienation could offer heuristically, as demonstrated for example by both his choice to work as a clerk for Sinzheimer and later on to write *Scientific Man vs Power Politics*, which put him deliberately at odds with, and in opposition to, the orthodoxy of American political science (Amstrup, 1978, p. 173; Scheuerman, 2009, p. 13). Alienation was for Morgenthau the conscious act of detachment that enabled him to analyze situations with greater rationality due to his enhanced capacity for intellectual synopsis (see also Loader, 1997, pp. 217–29; Barboza, 2006, pp. 232–55). This ability to rationalize is confirmed by several people who knew Morgenthau personally. George Eckstein, a distant relative of Morgenthau, noted that Morgenthau had a "very rational mind, always coolly alert to analyze and understand any given event or situation" (Eckstein, 1981, p. 641). Likewise, the jurist Richard Falk highlighted Morgenthau's "unflinching capacity for objectivity" (Falk, 1984, p. 77). Alienation also enabled Morgenthau to become aware of his own position and those of others. This not only allowed him to remark upon and to attempt to obviate distortions in his own thinking, but it also provided him with the capacity to detect and decipher nuances of politics as well as in the writing of others (Morgenthau, 1965, p. 81); as a reviewer remarked regarding Morgenthau's *The Purpose of American Politics*:

> Prof. Morgenthau's great advantage is that, as a scholar and citizen already mature, when he chose the United States as his country, he can look at it from within and also with the critical objectivity of an outsider. So he knows where the foundations, emotional and social, are weak. (HJM-Archive Box 144)

The power of dissent

The final concept on which Morgenthau's worldview rested, the development of which *The Concept of the Political* was a cornerstone in his understanding of scholarship as dissidence, is the power of dissent. The developments in Europe, culminating in the Second World War and in the Holocaust, reinforced Morgenthau's conviction that the political is the central aspect of society and that therefore active civic engagement is required to prevent the violation of a political and public sphere of free and discursive contestation.

Morgenthau was an eyewitness to the rise of the totalitarian national-socialist state. In the years of the 1920s and 30s, agitation and propaganda gradually mantled the political discourse with a total form of ideology. Through a discourse of exclusivity, uniqueness, discrimination, and racism, minorities were barred from society and the individual was attached to and subdued by the masses in his/her quest for identity. Shortly after Adolf Hitler was appointed Chancellor (January 30, 1933), on the "Day of Potsdam" (March 21, 1933), this discourse was already further historicized and visualized, and functioned as the means for identity creation through the seizure of the Prussian myth of Potsdam (Münkler, 2009, pp. 275–94) which was meant to put Hitler into direct line with Fredrick the Great, Otto von Bismarck, and Paul von Hindenburg. Arendt has noted that totalitarianism would have been a new form of government precisely because it would provide remedy for the modern feeling of meaninglessness and solitude by recreating identity within the totalitarian framework (Arendt, 1953, pp. 303–6). A republic was especially endangered by totalitarianism because other than in an absolute monarchy or theocracy, where the subjects are born into a transcendental order and do not have to question their identity, a republic required its citizens to create their identity by themselves. The specific danger of totalitarian regimes is that they claim to be deriving their existence and laws from natural and/or divine law (Arendt, 1953, pp. 306–10). It was this danger that Morgenthau had in mind when he was criticizing ideologies and emphasizing that the survival of a republic would be dependent upon its ideal of "embedded criticism" (Tjalve, 2008, p. 5).

Morgenthau's profound belief and worldview that the political, as the core of society, would need civic engagement was deeply seeded in his European experience. He was genuinely driven, first, by the apprehension that the political sphere of the Weimar Republic was in danger of being taken over by the racist ideology of national-socialism and, second, by witnessing this actually come to pass. This apprehension was in part fuelled by his belief that the majority of intellectuals would remain indifferent and inactive, maybe even unaware. Morgenthau believed this was demonstrated at a reception in the house of the jurist Karl Neumeyer in Munich in 1935. All the guests were critical towards national-socialism, yet, "[t]hey all argued against the Nazis from their own personal point of view". Morgenthau added that, after telling them about the execution of a befriended Jewish lawyer, they replied as follows: "Don't talk to us about this. We don't mix in politics... It doesn't interest us" (Postscript, 1984, pp. 363–4). Yet, it was only after the Second World War that Morgenthau became fully aware of the total nemesis – physical and moral – which totalitarianism can cause and he lived up to his ideal of engaged scholarship after his emigration.

After the enormous success of his textbook *Politics Among Nations* during the 1950s in the United States, Morgenthau's popularity rose to a level which made him a sought-after commentator; and he was eager to fill this role. Morgenthau published in several newspapers, such as the *New York Times* and *Washington Post* and liberal magazines, like *Commentary*, *Worldview*, and *New Republic*, commenting on topics including the Vietnam War, the rise of China, and student protests in the late 1960s. Furthermore, he supported the public's capacity to follow the opinion-making process by instructing the wider public on a local level. He worked, for example, for the Keneseth Israel Beth Shalom Congregation in Kansas City, during his time at the local university there from 1939–43, and also for the Adult Education Council of Greater Chicago until the late 1960s (HJM-Archive Boxes 3; 91). During this time, Morgenthau gave more than 60 public lectures and talks per year throughout the United States, which clearly indicates his enormous efforts to fulfill his ideal of civic engagement and critical public discourse (HJM-Archive Box 153). Morgenthau was also actively engaged in the public sphere by participating and heading countless civil rights associations, such as the Academic Committee on Soviet Jewry from 1969–79 (HJM-Archive Box 2). Certainly, the interest in facilitating the emigration of Soviet Jews can be explained by his own experience of being an emigrant (Mollov, 1997, pp. 561–75). Largely forgotten today, however, is his criticism of the Vietnam War. At that time, Morgenthau was probably one of its earliest critics (See, 2001, p. 424) and he became a "national figure" of resistance during the course of the war (Arendt and McCarthy, 1995).

Indeed, when Morgenthau was heard, he was often threatened for his civic engagement. Morgenthau's candidacy for the presidency of the American Political Science Association in the early 1970s was impeded and there is also evidence to suggest a "Project Morgenthau" under the Lyndon B. Johnson administration which involved collecting incriminating evidence against Morgenthau to publicly expose him (Cozette, 2008, p. 17). However, this could neither stop Morgenthau from his civic engagement nor from his participation in the public opinion-making process because

> [a] political science which is true to its moral commitment ought at the very least to be an unpopular undertaking. At its very best, it cannot help being a subversive and revolutionary force with regard to certain vested interests – intellectual, political, economic, social in general. For it must sit in continuous judgment upon political man and political society, measuring their truth, which is in good part a social convention, by its own. By doing so, it is not only an embarrassment to society intellectually, but it becomes also a political threat to the defenders or the opponents of the status quo or to both; for the social conventions about power, which political science cannot help subjecting to a critical – and often destructive – examination, are one of the main sources from which the claims to power, and hence power itself, derive. (Morgenthau, 1955, pp. 446–7)

Morgenthau had once witnessed how quickly a republic can be turned into a totalitarian state and he tried to prevent this happening again in the future.

2
Contextualization of "The Concept of the Political"

In the political and legal debates of his time

The Concept of the Political was written by Morgenthau in 1933 after his doctoral thesis, when he was already in Geneva to pursue his *Habilitation*. In many respects, it is a continuation of the questions that Morgenthau had analyzed in his doctoral thesis. In this earlier work from 1929, however, Morgenthau had realized that dispute and conflict settlement in international relations is not merely a juridical question, but a political one. Consequently, he had devoted some pages to the elaboration of the political; but only in *The Concept of the Political* a few years later was Morgenthau able to produce a coherent study on this topic. Thus, the years between his doctoral thesis and *The Concept of the Political* were primarily devoted to the elaboration of a concept of the political and its implications for the social sciences and humanities.[1]

The crisis of German "Staatslehre"

Despite being seemingly a by-product, *The Concept of the Political* is essential for the contextualization and understanding of Morgenthau's oeuvre and worldview since it provides a genuine expression of his ontological and epistemological commitments which informed all his later works. With this study, Morgenthau attempted to establish the political as the driving force of sociation and consequently as the key focus of the social sciences and humanities. What Morgenthau precisely understood as the political and how the concept of power feeds into his understanding of the political will be of further interest below; first, however, we have to investigate why Morgenthau attempted to establish the political as the focal point of the social sciences and humanities. In order to follow Morgenthau's aspirations, we must have a closer look at the inaugural lecture Morgenthau gave when he arrived in Geneva in 1932, one year prior to the publication of *The Concept of the Political*. In this lecture, entitled 'Der Kampf der deutschen Staatslehre um die Wirklichkeit des Staates' ('The Struggle of German "Staatslehre" about the Concept and Reality of the State'[2]) (Morgenthau, 1932), Morgenthau questioned and criticized the discipline of *Staatslehre*, as exemplified in the writings of Georg Jellinek, Hans Kelsen and Carl Schmitt, for its inability to provide a critical analysis of the cultural crisis, a crisis typical for modernity and most manifest in the decline of democratic culture in the Weimar Republic; a crisis that would have deprived humans of metaphysics instilling meaning into the conduct of human life, increased the ideologization of life and turned the nation-state into a 'blind and potent monster' (as he later described it; see Morgenthau, 1962a, p. 61).

By the time Morgenthau gave his inaugural lecture in Geneva, he had hoped that his academic years of travel would have come to an end. Soon thereafter, however, Morgenthau realized that anti-Semitism did not stop at borders. During the lecture, 'anti-Semitic German colleagues' (HJM-Archive Box 197) attempted to debase Morgenthau by questioning his intellectual capacity, and attendance at his lectures on German public law was low as numerous anti-Semitic German students refused to be taught by a Jew (Frei, 2001, p. 50). In addition to this anti-Semitic humiliation, Morgenthau soon also felt academically ostracized as his post-doctoral thesis was turned down by the examiners Walther Burckhardt and Paul Guggenheim in November 1933 (Frei, 2001, pp. 45–8; Jütersonke, 2010, pp. 78–9). Morgenthau felt particularly mistreated by Guggenheim's evaluation as Guggenheim attacked Morgenthau on personal grounds, even though the scholars had thus far been on good terms. Morgenthau countered Guggenheim's attack by writing several letters to the dean of the law faculty, Paul Logoz. After much debate Morgenthau eventually submitted his work to the prestigious Paris-based publisher Félix Alcan, hoping this would force the faculty to reconsider his case. Indeed, the acceptance of his manuscript for publication forced the faculty to appoint a new board of examiners. Among them was

Kelsen, who had shortly before arrived in Geneva after having been dismissed from his chair in Cologne. Kelsen was the right choice to assess Morgenthau's thesis because not only was he a senior scholar in *Staatslehre*, but Morgenthau's thesis was also largely a critical examination of Kelsen's legal positivism.

Thus, it was Kelsen to whom Morgenthau 'owed his *Habilitation* in Geneva', as Kelsen's biographer Rudolf Métall (1969, p. 64; also: Frei, 2001, pp. 48–9) confirms, *and* also eventually his subsequent academic career, because Kelsen produced the positive evaluation that convinced the board of examiners to award Morgenthau his *Habilitation*. Morgenthau remained grateful for this positive inter-vention throughout his lifetime and showed his gratitude to Kelsen on several occasions. As Morgenthau was already established in the United States by the time Kelsen arrived there in 1940, Morgenthau tried to promote Kelsen's scholarship, even making enquiries about potential job opportunities for Kelsen's son-in-law in the area around Kansas City, where Morgenthau was then teaching (HJM-Archive Box 11). Also, late in his life, Morgenthau recalled this stroke of good fortune and dedicated his collection of essays *Truth and Power* (1970) to Kelsen.

This personal affection, which is clearly evidenced in the correspon-dence retained at the Library of Congress, is not, however, reflected in an intellectual congruence. Morgenthau accepted Kelsen's legal positivism as a temporarily feasible solution for *Staatslehre* to deal with the effects of the cultural crisis since, through its partition from actual events, it was an attempt to rescue scholarly standards from ideologization. Still, Morgenthau criticized Kelsen because ultimately he could not have provided answers to the traditional questions of German *Staatslehre* which Morgenthau considered to be among the most fundamental questions of humankind. Kelsen would not have been concerned with questions regarding the exis-tence or value of governmental institutions and legal orders or their development and demise, nor would he have analyzed justifications of authority. However, people will strive to get meaningful expla-nations and justifications about the society they live in. They will aspire to make sense of their concrete circumstances of life. Legal positivism, however, would only provide abstract explanations of the legal framework (*Sollordnung*) to which the state would have been reduced to. This was, for Morgenthau, the cardinal error of Kelsen's legal positivism for it would omit the human factor in public law. However, such a human factor would be inevitable 'as long as the formation of the public reality remains the subject of emotional contentions. Until then it is impossible to think about the state, whose existence is tied to one's own destiny, without making judgments about and ascribing meaning to public affairs' (Morgenthau, 1932a, p. 17; translation by the authors). Therefore, Morgenthau renounced Kelsen's legal positivism as not being able to depict the real image of human affairs.

Equally, Schmitt was criticized by Morgenthau in his inaugural lecture, despite the fact that there was an initial agreement between them based on their mutual belief that the core of any process of sociation was the political. As early as 1930 Morgenthau emphasized that this would be because politics is the realm in which diverse human interests collide and the basis from which dominant social and political institutions would emerge (Morgenthau, 1930c, p. 2). A similar argument was made in Schmitt's version of *The Concept of the Political* in which he remarked that the political would be a prerequisite of the state (Schmitt, 1996, p. 19). As William Scheuerman remarked, this congruence is due to amendments Schmitt made to his previous essay with the same title from 1927 after Morgenthau had sent him a copy of his doctoral thesis. Previously, Schmitt had pursued a concept of power politics which was unrestricted by normative influence and which could be distinguished from other societal realms such as economics (Scheuerman, 2007, p. 510).

This incidence has triggered – in Jütersonke's words – a whole 'Morgenthau–Schmitt "cottage industry"' (Jütersonke 2010, p. 66) as we find references to it in the works of numerous scholars, such as Pichler (1998), Scheuerman (1999, 2009), Koskenniemi (2000, 2004) and Williams (2004) to name just the most well known. This evolving Morgenthau–Schmitt discourse is, indeed, to a certain extent in accordance with the facts as Morgenthau did get engaged in the 1920s with the work of Schmitt. As a student and an aspiring legal scholar Morgenthau had to engage with Schmitt, who was one of the doyens of the field. This is clearly evidenced in Morgenthau's inaugural lecture in which he critically examined the works of three of the most recent towering figures in the field. Morgenthau (1984, p. 16) readily acknowledged this late in his life. Yet, as students of International

Relations, we should not forget that Schmitt's elaboration of the concept of the political was not the first of its kind. Other scholars before him in the field of *Staatslehre*, like Rudolf Smend, worked on the importance of this concept. This is why this engagement with Schmitt should not lead to an assumption that Morgenthau was positively influenced by him; rather the only assertion which can be made is that there was a reverse process of intellectual stimulation, as recent scholarship has shown (Jütersonke, 2010; Rösch, 2011). The reader of the present edition of *The Concept of the Political* – the only time Morgenthau ever substantially dealt with Schmitt, apart from a later, however, unpublished German translation (1934–35) of the relevant part of *The Concept of the Political* – will easily recognize that Morgenthau deplored Schmitt's understanding of the political on moral and conceptual grounds.

Morgenthau's initial agreement with Schmitt that the political is the core of society, was promptly contradicted by Morgenthau because he could not agree with Schmitt's belligerent conceptualization of the political, to wit, that '[t]he specific political distinction to which political actions and motives can be reduced is that between friend and enemy [foe]' (Schmitt, 1996, p. 26). Morgenthau not only criticized Schmitt for his lack of morality, but he also criticized his conceptual framework since he considered Schmitt's reduction of the political to friend and foe as tautological. Morgenthau argued that love and hate would be psychological attributes of particular people, reflected in personal beliefs and tastes, and would not be sufficient to distinguish the political realm (Morgenthau, 1933, pp. 52–3). Therefore, the distinction between friend and foe would be politically tautological because both friend and foe could be of political value (*wertvoll*) just as much as both could also be politically of no value at all (*wertlos*) (Morgenthau, 1934–35, p. 5). What is more, Morgenthau would have agreed with Harald Kleinschmidt's assessment that this tautology characterized a more general problem in Schmitt: he would have decided on friend and foe at his sole discretion. Indeed, Schmitt would have assessed existing norms in correspondence to the 'meta-standard' of his own values (Kleinschmidt, 2004, p. 17). This is why Morgenthau claimed that this dichotomy would not be relevant for scholarly purposes to distinguish politics from other social aspects (Morgenthau, 1932).

As the above-mentioned definition of the political from his doctoral thesis has shown, Morgenthau had a very different understanding of the political in comparison to Schmitt because he argued that the political has no fixed substance, but is a quality or coloring (*Färbung*). 'A question which is of political nature today, can be bereft of any political meaning tomorrow' (Morgenthau, 1929, p. 67, translation by the authors.). This means that the political occurred for Morgenthau when humans pursued their interests through dialogue. Any issue or substance can become political as soon as people take an increased interest in it. Morgenthau operated on the assumption that this pursuit of interests in collectivity is part of human nature, as he elaborated in the above-mentioned unpublished manuscript on the 'Derivation of the Political from the Nature of Man' from 1930. It is part of human nature because only through this pursuit can the involved parties reassure themselves of their own strengths and capabilities and gain meaning about their own self. This, what Morgenthau perceived to be a natural collective pursuit of interests, eventually provided people with power. Power was, therefore, the defining aspect of the political that set it apart from other social realms. As we will see in the last part of this introduction (Chapter 4), Morgenthau had a complex, two-dimensional understanding of power. He distinguished between an empirical concept of power, understood as the capacity to dominate, and a normative notion of power, understood as the will to work together and create something valuable for them.

Special attention within Morgenthau's criticism of Carl Schmitt should further be paid to his dismissal of dualistic thinking, as it was inherent to Schmitt's conceptualization of the political. Morgenthau views Schmittian dualism as a legacy of Hegelian philosophy, as can be deduced from a brief comment in an endnote.[3] As Morgenthau argues (and as shown above), Schmitt's concept and its underlying premises were metaphysical in character and, so the argument proceeds, could only be countered by a likewise metaphysical concept *or* with a demonstration of its inner contradictions. Since Morgenthau refused to develop or to invoke (another) metaphysics himself, his criticism emphasized inner contradictions in Schmitt. One of those contradictions, according to Morgenthau, consists in the mode of dualist thinking and its dichotomist categories of 'good' and 'evil', 'beautiful' and 'ugly' etc. Further to the fact that these moralistic, aesthetic, etc. categories were at the complete discretion of the one who introduced and used them, and were for this reason alone ripe for dismissal (see above), Morgenthau also saw here an *epistemological* problem: that of how the object of research is constituted.

At the same time and congruent with his criticism of Schmitt, Morgenthau asserts that this epistemological problem, even if it is a problem of a theoretical (*'wissenschaftstheoretischer'*) nature with certain practical consequences, is, however, not a 'real' or 'objective' one; rather, it was constructed and (self)produced.[4] This is so because there is no 'reality' – that is, no 'real' object of experience and research beyond the realm of attention given to those phenomena which lie within the reach and focus of those categories themselves; or which are made to fall within, are subsumed into and subjected to respective realms. This problem of tautology (see also above) – that is, that the research object is constituted by the categories the researcher has in mind and which he/she uses to subjugate reality, which itself (re)constitutes the focus of the researcher, but which is nothing but a reproduction and affirmation of his/her initial categories – applies to aesthetics, morality, religion, economy and, ultimately, politics.

This problem of tautology and of the confinement of research objects (ultimately of objectivity as understood by Morgenthau; see more on that below) has a further, more profound dimension which is not discussed by Morgenthau, but which is inherent in his problematization and in his discussions. This is the problem of reification and objectification of 'reality' due to, and according to, *a priori* categories.[5] Ultimately, it is these categories themselves that *become* 'the' reality; or, better yet, what is perceived to be real/reality is so only because of, and according to, the categories applied. Not only is this a submission, seizure and confinement of 'reality' by and according to those categories, the status of which is only one of *a priori* production without any reflection in the world – that is, they are mere products of the mind – it is also an epistemological restriction of human perceptions and representations of 'reality' and their experiences, as well as of their agency in this 'reality'.[6] In all these regards, the potentially multiple forms and possibilities of reality in historical, cultural, societal, individual etc. terms and the likewise multiple and endless forms of our agency towards and our representations of those forms are restricted and shaped along the lines of dualistic categories. Not only is this an injustice to all divergent forms of humanity and political and social order (historical, cultural etc.),[7] but it further limits humankind's optionalities to act socially and politically in this world. It restricts humankind's spectrum of action towards the problems of war and peace, the regulation of conflicts and disputes, as well as action in diplomacy, in humankind's engagement in the public sphere and the creation of order, and in foreign policy: all core themes in Morgenthau's political science. Political action, following the predetermined schemes of dualistic and dichotomist categories, is necessarily blind towards alternative approaches that lie beyond these categories. In opposition to these kinds of epistemologically induced reductions and seizures, Morgenthau would unreservedly endorse the normative understanding of political optionality in Arendt,[8] as evidenced by his own similar wording in *The Concept of the Political*: 'spheres of elasticity' as a core requirement of the political.[9]

Contextualization in the current (late 20th and 21st centuries) debates of politics and International Relations

As a thematic continuation of his 1932 inaugural lecture at the University of Geneva, called 'Der Kampf der deutschen Staatslehre um die Wirklichkeit des Staates' ('The Struggle of German "Staatslehre" about the Concept and Reality of the State'), Morgenthau's *Concept of the Political* represents his continuing search for the concept of the state and the political. He perceives such a concept as lying somewhere in the middle ground between, at the one end of the intellectual spectrum of German "*Staatslehre*" during the Weimar Republic, Hans Kelsen's legal positivism and, at the other end, Carl Schmitt's concept of the political as the dualism between friend and foe. However, as we have seen above, Morgenthau criticized both Kelsen's legal positivism and Schmitt's dualism. He refused Kelsen for his exclusion of political questions from theoretical reflection due to the supremacy of legal formalism and the chimera of the justiciability of every social and 'political' dispute; and he condemned Schmitt's dualism for its binary epistemology and his amoralism. And, contemporaneously to criticizing both, he was experiencing the downfall of the Weimar Republic while drafting his *Concept of the Political*, which was published in 1933 when Hitler seized power in Germany.

Academically speaking, Morgenthau attributes great responsibility for this downfall to the limitations of the theoretical conceptualizations of politics and the state in the German social sciences and particularly in *"Staatslehre"* as represented in both Kelsen's and Schmitt's works. And he feels his criticism being (tragically) confirmed by history. Thus, Morgenthau's major attempts in this early book must be seen in his effort, *first*, to separate the legal from the political sphere – or, to put it differently, to free political deliberation from legal regulation – and to establish the political as something distinct; and, *second*, to normatively conceptualize the political, and accordingly, the task of the state as the creation of "spheres of elasticity" (from his *Concept of the Political*; see below Part II) – that is, as the political norm of a critical, contesting public sphere and space for the peaceful "antagonism of interests",[10] which was initially drafted by Morgenthau in general terms and would then translate into the international.

When Morgenthau criticizes Kelsen and Schmitt (for all the reasons discussed) and in critical disassociation from both develops his concept of the political, including the political norms of elasticity and deliberative competition, we see the beginning of the development of two particular characteristics of his political thoughts. *First*, a set of epistemological commitments running throughout his oeuvre of which the most important is the spatio-temporal contingency of political theory, knowledge and political order;[11] and, *second*, strongly interrelated with the first, we see the emergence of his intellectual (and at times also political) fight for the humanization of politics and the repoliticization of the public sphere. These claims find their target in, and protest against, a series of developments of modern politics and society, such as social planning and engineering, positivism, liberalism as a political ideology, scientism and the scientification of the humanities, and the bureaucratization of the modern state. Very interesting in this regard is his correspondence from the early 1960s with Gottfried Karl Kindermann, then Professor of International Politics at the University of Munich and a former PhD student of Morgenthau, about the preparation of a collected paper edition of Morgenthau's main articles in German.[12] In this letter Morgenthau suggested the following sub-chapter headline: "Realism as revolt against historical optimism".[13]

Morgenthau's epistemological commitments shall be discussed in greater detail below.[14] His academic and political fight for the humanization of politics and the repoliticization of the public sphere provide the most important feature for contextualizing Morgenthau's oeuvre and his *Concept of the Political* in contemporary – that is, late 20th- and 21st-century – debates in the humanities and social sciences in general and Politics and International Relations in particular. By this contextualization we recognize the intellectual and conceptual proximity between the oeuvre of Morgenthau and what can be called "classical realism" more generally and two other movements which are usually seen as separate, if not even opposite to Morgenthau's political thought and realism. These two movements are critical theory and post-structuralist theory. This said, it does not mean that *classical realism* as represented in Morgenthau, *critical theory* as represented in Theodor W. Adorno, Max Horkheimer and Herbert Marcuse, as well as Hannah Arendt, and *post-structuralist theory*[15] would have found and elaborated the same theorems responding to problems of modern society and politics; it does mean, however, that they were and are all concerned with the same *problématiques* of modern politics, based partly on the same historical experience and also on the fact that they therefore ask and asked the same questions, elaborating congruent analyses and agendas, even if these differ in detail and theoretico-political conclusions.

The problématique, which these movements and schools commonly perceive(d) to exist in modern society and politics and which many of their representatives experienced as *scholars émigré* in the United States during the years of National Socialism in Germany, can be summarized as the increasing rationalization and scientification of society and politics under the influences of modern reason and positivism. Respective forms of social engineering would lead to the de-humanization of politics and society as well as to forms of totalitarian bureaucratization, social planning, and unrestricted capitalist logicalities as most significantly manifest in the ideologies of consumerism and growth. From these analyses critical of modernity, which are more or less congruent between, and play a paramount role in, classical realism, critical theory, and post-structuralist argumentation, academic and political agendas flow which request and engage *the moral reconstruction of humane politics*. Although this target is theorized differently and very divergent forms of engagement are developed, this common analytical and *critical* focus is supported by another joint conceptual emphasis. Though in different termi- nologies and philosophical languages, we find throughout the wide range of classical realist, critical theory, and post-structuralist writ- ings the emphasis on the return of the human and of humanity into political and social order and its theorizations. Hand-in-hand with this emphasis goes the request for the repoliticization of the public sphere, which is seen as being destroyed by bureaucratic and eco- nomic rationalities.

As will be seen below,[16] this fundamental appreciation of the human condition[17] of political and social order, accompanied by modernity-critical analyses according to which this human condi- tion has been destroyed by modern, rational, and positivist rational- ities, is manifest in Morgenthau in the prominence of his concept of power, particularly in its normative dimension envisioning power as the peaceful, public deliberation of antagonistic interests. As stated before, although this Morgenthauian response does differ from the responses of, for example, Herbert Marcuse, Hannah Arendt, and Jenny Edkins,[18] the responses meet, however, in their demand for the return of humanity and politics into public life, based on the critical analysis of their destruction and annihilation through the "totalitarian tendency" of technological and bureaucratic control – most dangerously and tragically becoming reality during National Socialism and epitomized in the Holocaust, but also continuing to occur under the advanced industrial and capitalist societies of the West. As Marcuse most clearly indicates:

> As the project unfolds, it shapes the entire universe of discourse and action, intellectual and material culture. In the medium of technology, culture, politics, and the economy merge into an omnipresent system which swallows up or repulses all alter- natives. The productivity and growth potential of this system stabilize the society and contain technical progress within the framework of domination. Technological rationality has become political rationality. (1964, p. 6)

Morgenthau would have unreservedly endorsed and voiced this critique and analysis. Moreover, there seems to be overlapping con- gruence between Morgenthau and Marcuse's diagnostic of modernity when he elaborates this analysis into the argument of the one-dimensional man in his academic best-seller with the same title.[19] And, as well known, Adorno and Horkheimer shape this paradox (and quandary) between total domination and (the promise) of human politics and liberty as relation between myth and enlightenment, which they find most explicitly and authoritatively elaborated in Homer's *Odyssey* and *Iliad*. They note:

> The most primitive myth already contains the element of false-hood that triumphs in the fraudulence of fascism, a deceitfulness that fascism imputes to enlightenment. No work, however, gives more eloquent testimony to the entwinement of enlightenment and myth than the Odyssey, the fundamental text of European civilization. In Homer, epic and myth, form and subject matter do not so much diverge from each other as, rather, confront and define one another. The aesthetic dualism attests to the historical-philosophical tendency. (1992, p. 111)[20]

Certainly Morgenthau shares this "tragic vision of politics" (as Richard Lebow terms it (2003); see most explicitly, Morgenthau, 1945b), which consists in the fundamental tragedy of humankind not being able to escape the human condition of death, transience, and mortality, however hard and desperately one may try. There is even the paradox that the more frantically and passionately humans try to overcome their conditions – and at some point may even presume to have done so successfully, as did Icarus – the deeper they fall and the greater the disaster caused. Not only is it impossible to overcome these conditions, however, it is likewise just as impossible to ignore them. This kind of ignorance would result in hubris in one's conduct of life and political agency. In this fundamental view of human life and political and social agency, which Morgenthau expressed in his writings as early as 1930(b) in "Der Selbstmord mit gutem Gewissen" ("Suicide with a Good Conscience") (though this manuscript was unpublished), we find the fundamental worldview behind his critique of idealism as an epistemological position and a political ideology. Just as Adorno and Horkheimer invoke Greek mythology in Homer, Morgenthau refers to figures like William Shakespeare's Richard III or Don Juan, as well as to narrations such as Aristophanes's *Symposium* in order to evoke tragic figures and motifs of either hubris towards or ignorance of humanity's captivity in social and political conditions.[21]

Not less explicit nor less fundamental in her modernity critique and in her analysis of the loss of humanity through capitalist rationalities is Arendt – the lifelong friend and colleague of Morgenthau at the University of Chicago and later at the New School in New York – in her book with the symptomatic (and well-chosen) title *The Human Condition* (1958). It describes the reduction of humankind's anthropological constitution – which she derives from an Aristotelian vision of political ethics[22] – from a three-dimensional capacity of Being to a one-dimensional *animal laborans*.[23] According to Aristotle (and Arendt), human existence would be characterized by his/her faculties to labor, to work, and to action and speech. Among these, action and speech are the genuinely political faculties while labor and work would belong to the social and economic world (to the *oikos*). Through technological progress and capitalist modes of production humans have come to be dominated by labor – being thus developed into an *animal laborans* – while at the same time humans have lost their genuine political modes of existence, namely acting and deliberating in the public and political sphere regarding the principles of humankind's common good and its political order. Thus, humankind would have lost its human condition which is bound to public action and speech and could only be recovered through a repoliticization – that is, open and free deliberation – of the fundamental normative principles of order and togetherness. The domination of human life by techniques and rationalities of labor (capitalism) and modern bureaucracy is, according to Arendt – and here we have another commonality with Marcuse and Morgenthau – not only totalitarian in that it seizes the human condition and destroys humanity, but also in that it presents forms of violence. She writes in "Reflections on Violence":

> Finally, the greater the bureaucratization of public life, the greater will be the attraction of violence. In a fully developed bureaucracy there is nobody left with whom one could argue, to whom one could present grievances, on whom the pressures of power could be exerted. Bureaucracy is the form of government in which everybody is deprived of political freedom, of the power to act; for the rule by Nobody is not no-rule, and where all are equally powerless we have a tyranny without a tyrant. (1969, p. 18)

A third and most colorful and important theoretical movement in the discipline of International Relations, which evinces the joint horizon with classical realism and critical theory of problematizing and critiquing modernity as well as arguing for a return of humanity and the political, is post-structuralist theory. This becomes perhaps most obvious in the writings of Jenny Edkins which signify and suggest this common concern and agenda. Edkins understands post-structuralism explicitly as a movement that is committed to repoliticizing politics, since in modern western societies the political would have been gradually removed through positivist social planning and engineering (Edkins, 1999). Whether, or not, post-structuralism achieved this aspiration is not the question here, but it is important to briefly outline what she regards as *de-politicization* and the reasons for it.

Edkins distinguishes between politics and the political: a distinction Morgenthau would have endorsed. Politics is defined by her as the realm of the institutionalized execution of government. Elections, political parties, the Executive, Judiciary and Legislature, diplomacy, war and international treaties would all be part of politics (Edkins, 1999, p. 2). What is commonly called politics would be, therefore, closely linked to the idea of the sovereign state (Edkins, 1999, p. 2), as, for example, Jellinek's general theory of the state in which he distinguished between national territory, people and authority. Politics is perceived to be the realm in which the government would have the means to execute authority within a certain area over a certain number of people, entitled by mutual recognition from other states. Post-structuralism, however, argues, according to Edkins, that the idea of sovereignty leads to a de-politicization within the realm of sovereign politics and the (Westphalian) international system of nation-states.

By referring to examples of humanitarian aid and securitization Edkins provides an argument that Morgenthau made 30 years before (Morgenthau, 1973). Particularly, technologization will have allowed states to de-politicize politics because it will have provided them with the means, on the one hand, to deprive people of the possibilities to criticize government decisions, hence to fulfill their role as citizens, and, on the other hand, to create a substitute for the political through ideologies and commodities (Edkins, 1999, pp. 9–14). Paul Hirst provided a further explanation as to why de-politicization occurred. He considered the very system of nation-states as an act of de-politicization because, internally, the idea of sovereignty will have permitted states to reduce, if not remove, conflicts and antagonisms from the realm of politics. This will have enabled states to build other forms of identification through ideology in order to create homogeneity and compliance within the state. Externally, however, states will have created a self-fulfilling prophecy by putting the focus on the primacy of the reason of the state. This will have led to the consideration of international relations as a question 'of the balance of power and the acquisition of territory in Europe and colonies abroad' (Hirst, 2001, p. 57). On the same ground, in 1979 Morgenthau came to the conclusion that 'we are living in a dream world' (Morgenthau, 1979, p. 42) because international politics and International Relations are still operating on the out-dated concept of the nation-state.

Post-structuralism, so Edkins continues to argue – unfortunately without referring to anything beyond the triad of phenomenology, psychoanalysis and critical theory – therefore found its rationale as a movement to counter this de-politicization and to bring the political back. The political is defined by Edkins as having 'to do with the establishment of that very social order which sets out a particular, historically specific account of what counts as politics' (1999, p. 2). The political would be the moment when a new social and political order is created, regardless of what this new order looks like. Hence, there would be uncertainty among its creators about the final objectification of this order, but it would be also a moment of openness characterized by a dispute of its creators as they all attempt to reify their social and political ideals. The political would be, therefore, quintessentially a moment when people came together and acted in their quest to establish some form of social and political order (Edkins, 1999, pp. 7–9). In this regard, Morgenthau, and also Arendt (to whom Edkins does not refer), went even a step further because the political was for them not only a singular moment, but the *constant* requirement for democracy and humane politics as a permanent process – as expressed by Richard Ashley and R. B. J. Walker (and in implicit opposition to Edkins):

> Here, where identity is *always* in process … the limits authored by one or another sovereign standpoint can be questioned and

transgressed ... and new cultural resources can be cultivated ... Here it becomes possible to explore, generate, and circulate new [and] always *dissident* ways of thinking, doing, and being political. (1990, p. 263; italics by the authors)

The analogy between classical realist/Morgenthauian and post-structuralist thinking can be furthered with reference to Richard Ashley's and Rob Walker's paper (just referenced) on 'Speaking the Language of Exile: Dissident Thought in International Studies' (1990). In this paper, Ashley and Walker investigate political and disciplinary sites of exile and dissidence against the modern political narratives of sovereignty, territory, identity, and reason. They characterize these sites as follows: 'In these sites ... identity is never sure, community is always uncertain, meaning is always in doubt' (1990, p. 261). This characterization of fundamental patterns of thought in large parts of current, post-structuralist International Relations scholarship resembles the three *'weltanschauliche'* ("worldview") motifs of the disenchantment of the world, the power of dissent, and the conscious pariah in Morgenthau as elaborated above.[24] One may conclude from these similarities and resemblances that much of the critique of post-structuralist theorists of large (nearly all) parts of historical theory (beyond phenomenology, psychoanalysis, and critical theory – and writings *within the same* theorems) and of classical realism (and Morgenthau in particular) appears as a *Don Quichottian* fight against windmills – that is, as unnecessary and inappropriate criticism. Much effort could have been spared here and synergies could have been accomplished through more profound and serious reception of, as well as conjuncture and less generalizing rejections and even hostilities against, theories and theoreticians beyond the streams mentioned above (in other words the rather large body of theories and theoreticians that are also critical of, and in dissidence towards, modern political narratives of sovereignty, territory, identity, reason, and progress). Why try to reinvent the wheel when there are theorems (*not* 'theories') in place which are already well rolling, and which could be rediscovered and referred to in a constructive sense were their questions and concerns acknowledged?[25]

The previous discussions show mainly the following: it is becoming abundantly clear – and it will get increasingly clear as this

Introduction proceeds – that Morgenthau's (and we would argue in 'classical realism' general's) concern(s) and his approach to problematizing, thematizing, and answering those concerns are fundamentally different and even diametrically opposed to all kinds of neo-realist and neo-liberal approaches to the study of politics and International Relations. There are no justifiable and legitimate reasons for any identification of Morgenthau and classical realism with what has been called *"neo"*-realism (initially by Robert Keohane).[26] This non-unity between (classical) realism and "neo"-realism has, however, further implications which are particularly relevant for the study of knowledge formation in the discipline of International Relations. Thus, we conclude, that Morgenthau became trapped twice: he was embraced by an IR mainstream which positioned itself in a manipulated narrative of "realism", including a misread Morgenthauian legacy; and he was largely chosen as a/the wrong 'enemy' by post-structuralist theorists.

Under such a sociology of knowledge-perspective, it becomes obvious that the point of view which sees a steady progress in knowledge creation in the discipline, simultaneous to its history and existence as a discipline, is one of the 'myths' (according to Cynthia Weber) pervading the discipline and upholding its mainstream. There is neither a teleology of knowledge (production) nor some unfolding universal reason in the discipline; nor is there a development of increasingly profound insights into, and findings relating to, the dynamics of politics and political agency; nor is there something like complete knowledge: a chimera for Morgenthau.[27] There are, in fact, only *problématiques*, concerns and questions which may be shared among some and not shared by others. Those who share concerns may develop similar thoughts, approaches and eventual agendas even if (some) representatives are not aware of these links and this overlapping. And there are only genealogies of questions raised and genealogies of knowledge formation, rather than progress and teleology: receptions, interpretations, readings, writings, appropriations, etc. are attempts to understand, critically interpret, illuminate, and explicate the human, social, and political world in order to act upon it in a humane way. These are contingencies of knowledge and political practices that do not comply with, and may even threaten, modern narratives of historical necessities and presumably authoritative cores of the discipline. This, however, is again a very Morgenthauian (and maybe critical theorist and obviously post-structuralist) think-ing and as such finds itself in contradiction and dissidence to the positivist idea of intellectual progress, advancement, and improve-ment by some "sovereign" reason penetrating and manifesting in the discipline: in short, it finds itself to be a "revolt against historical optimism" as Morgenthau argued.

3
Morgenthau's Epistemological Commitments

Morgenthau's criticism of rationalism, empiricism, and idealism

Reflecting upon Morgenthau's epistemology as it is communicated in *The Concept of the Political* and for the development of which this piece of writing is a milestone in Morgenthau's oeuvre, we recognize his critical disassociation from three theories of knowledge.[1] First, he is critical about a rationalist approach to overcome the confinements of human knowledge through the construction of knowledge of the external world out of indubitable principles possessed inherently by the mind itself, the most indubitable of such principles being Descartes's *"Cogito ergo sum"*. This kind of rationalist knowledge would be invulnerable to any kind of skepticism and is supposed to represent the basis of all further knowledge and derivations about the world.[2] We recognize here the belief that the existence of objects outside the self can be based on and deduced from the mind's awareness of its own existence, thereby allowing one to dispel all doubts and insecurities about knowledge, and accomplish epistemological security[3] regarding the existence, constitution, and character of the world (also called "dualism"; see Holt et al., 1960, p. 154). Morgenthau promotes a position that is critical about this epistemological paradigm and its *a priori*, experience-independent claims and assumptions about the world. Political realism in Morgenthau is hence an anti-Cartesian position which recognizes the mind-independent existence of an empirical world and human agency within this world, but which does not, however, claim secure and definite knowability, intellectual disposability or analytical accessibility of this world. His realism is aware that there exist factualities about the world and its penetrating principles that are *mind-independent*, but that those "facts" and principles, *however*, adopt different empirical meanings throughout history and cultures; they are conditioned and shaped by time and space-contingent constellations created through the human mind, perception, imagination, and agency.[4] As we will see below, this epistemological position has enormous effects on the study of politics in that it recognizes perennial forces which penetrate political reality, but requires for their understanding context-specific explanations and hermeneutic methods – in short, it is *"Erfahrungswissenschaft"* and thus proclaims universal epistemological positions and heuristic tools while at the same time demanding temporally and spatially sensitive explanations of particular manifestations of those perennial forces.

Second, Morgenthau is also averse to an empiricism which would base knowledge and justified beliefs about the (political) world on merely sensually conceived impressions and which would rely, in its assertions about the existence, constitution, and character of the world, on (ostensibly) mind-independent, *data bruta* – that is, methodologically on positivist quantification and measurement of social and political phenomena – built on the hope that through inductive logic there may be some kind of spill-over from data collection to knowledge. It is in this context of empiricism, paired with positivist methodology, that political science would have to be set apart from what is also called "naïve realism", which is described as follows: "The theory of naïve realism ... conceives of objects as directly presented to consciousness and being precisely what they appear to be ... they are themselves directly presented ... things *are* just what they *seem*" (Holt et al., 1960, p. 152).

And third, Morgenthau's epistemology, because it recognizes the mind-independent, however spatio-temporally qualified status of things real, "strips mind of its pretensions, but not of its value or greatness ... Realism dethrones the mind, [and at the same time] recognizes mind as chief in the world" (Alexander, 1960, p. 186). We here further recognize an anti-idealist position against the belief in a "world in which there exist only minds ... According to [this theory] ... the world of objects capable of existing independently of a knower ... is ... rejected" (Holt et al., 1960, pp. 154–5). Politically speaking, and in sharp contrast to Morgenthau's position, idealism would presume the fabricability and shapability of the world and of political strategies therein without, as he argues, taking into account to a sufficiently high degree the concepts of power, interest and morality and the "factual", but empirically divergent, constellations, which these concepts make cognizable. He notes:

> For realism, theory consists in ascertaining facts and giving them meaning through reason. It assumes that the character of a foreign policy can be ascertained only through the examination of the political acts performed and of the foreseeable consequences of these acts ... Yet examination of the facts is not enough. To give meaning to the factual raw material of foreign policy [here, we recognize Friedrich Nietzsche's "facts are stupid"[5]], we must approach political reality with a kind of rationale outline, a map that suggests to us ... possible meanings of foreign policy. (Morgenthau, from the first of his "Six Principles ... ", 1954)

This "map"[6] for the rational (and very purposefully Morgenthau does *not* write rationalist) conceptualization of reality is provided by the *concepts* of power, interest, and morality and their interplay. These concepts, which condensate in his mantra "interest defined in terms of power" (Morgenthau, from the second of his "Six Principles ... ", 1960), are such a rational conceptualization. They do not express an ontological statement of how the world "is", even if they became read, or rather misread, as such by International Relations mainstream time and again. In Morgenthau's words, they can also be understood as a "signpost that helps political realism to find its way through the landscape of international politics" (ibid.). Here it becomes clear that this sentence does *not* claim to represent reality, nor does it claim power, interest, and morality as *being* reality; rather it articulates epistemological categories which "provide the link between reason trying to understand international politics and the facts to be understood" (ibid.). And this is precisely not a subordination of political reality under *either* rationalist principles that would claim knowability or assumability of political reality as in "neo"-"realism" and its Cartesian legacies of "scientific knowledge"; *or* under empiricist measurements and quantifications as in positivist methodologies and their enthronement of methodology over theory; *or* under idealist beliefs in the produceability of political reality, an epistemological position which, according to Morgenthau, has the tendency to lead in its political consequences to moral crusade(r)s. Another quote in this context is also instructive in terms of the epistemological character of the concepts of power and interest: "The *concept* of interest defined as power imposes *intellectual discipline* upon the observer" (emphasis by the authors; Morgenthau, from the second of his "Six Principles... ", 1960).[7]

In order to further understand epistemology in Morgenthau – and it seems that he understood "realism" as epistemology, *not* as an ontology of international politics as often misread[8] – we need to emphasize his statements that empiricist and positivist accounts which would recruit some *data bruta* about the social and political word as if they had inherent meaning and could speak for themselves, while assuming that the more data were collected (i.e., the bigger the databases), the more knowledge one would possess and the more problems could be tackled, would indeed "become a pretentious collection of trivialities" (1962a, p. 27). He insists that empirics has to be given social and political meaning (Morgenthau, from the first of his "Six Principles... ", 1954) and that, as he notes elsewhere and much earlier (in 1951; here 1962a), "the empiricist commitment of modern political science to practical ends [i.e., as a 'problem-solving' empiricist science]... has powerfully contributed to its decline as theory" (1962a, p. 25). This criticism resonates with his argumentation against analogies between natural and social sciences and humanities, arguing that "(to) make susceptibility to quantitative measurement the yardstick of the scientific character of the social sciences in general and political science in particular is to deprive these sciences of that very orientation which is adequate to the understanding of their subject matter" (1962a, p. 27).

It is obvious that these arguments vehemently targeted scientism and increasing scientification of American political science in the 1940s and 50s, and thus were against the emerging mainstream in the discipline of which the sub-discipline of International Relations was by no way exempted. But what would be epistemologically adequate? We can understand Morgenthau's epistemology as a middle-ground between empiricism and rationalism when he notes:

> While it is unnecessary to argue the case for the need for factual information, it ought to be no more necessary to argue that

> factual description is not science, but a mere ... preparation for the
> scientific understanding of the facts. (1962a, p. 26)

Therefore, realist epistemology consists in the acknowledgment of the existence of mind-independent political realities in which, however, the mind plays a paramount role in that these mind-independent realities become meaningful *only through* theoretical understanding. Further to this, these "facts" *are not to be seen as eternally the same*, but have to be recognized in their spatio-temporal constellations.[9] This fundamental position of realist epistemology posits that both the thing-being-observed and the observer mutually influence and constitute each other in (the world of) social sciences. Though this position is anything but new, as it had been voiced by many post-positivist criticisms, it is nevertheless to be acknowledged that this mutual constitution of observer and the thing-being-observed was something self-evident for Morgenthau who was familiarized with this epistemological position through readings of Friedrich Nietzsche, Wilhelm Dilthey, Georg Simmel, Alfred Schütz, and Karl Mannheim.[10] To a certain extent therefore, post-positivist and post-structuralist as well as constructivist epistemological criticisms of positivist science can be found in Morgenthau – and with him in a comprehensive cosmos and tradition of continental-European phenomenological and hermeneutic social sciences and humanities.[11] Even if these traditions in Morgenthau appear to be ignored as forms of intellectual and academic resistance against positivist (i.e., empiricist and rationalist) epistemologies by large parts of International Relations scholarship, these traditions are valuable sources to connect to for every anti-positivist critique recognizing their value in the sociological and intellectual history of knowledge (production) in the social sciences, humanities and in International Relations.

However, what is further communicated by Morgenthau's epistemology is that the mutually constitutive relations between the observer and the things-being-observed, as well as the spatio-temporally varying political constellations, which all speak fundamentally against eternal entities in and of the socio-political world, hit some form of perennial (i.e., mind- and observer-independent) factors which it would be naïve not to take into account while both theorizing about, and acting in, political reality; and to ignore these factors would be as wrong as any exclusively positivist social science. We identify here also the anti-idealist epistemological position of realism. But what are those perennial factors and mind-independent realities? This question points to the human condition of politics.

The human condition of politics

If we reconsider Morgenthau's fundamental episteme of the recognition of mind-independent realities (or rather, mind-independent aspects of reality), the question arises regarding what this exactly means. A metaphor used by Morgenthau points to political anthropology as he writes in the second of his "Six Principles..." :

> The difference between international politics as it actually is and a rational theory derived from it is like the difference between a photograph and a painted portrait. The photograph shows everything that can be seen by the naked eye; the painted portrait does not show everything..., but it shows, or at least seeks to show, one thing that the naked eye cannot see: the human essence of the person portrayed. (Morgenthau, from the second of his "Six Principles...", 1960)

This metaphor suggests that a photograph would show, represent and make visible political reality as it were, whereas the painting would lose out compared to the photograph in terms of the resolution of the object portrayed. However, the painting would add a new aspect which the photo would not (be able to) show: Morgenthau calls it "the human essence", also "human nature", and we can translate this into human imagination and agency and their impact on, and constitution of, political reality. It is about political theory and the conceptual perspectives applied to decipher this component and its impact, both of which neither representation and description nor (*a priori*) rationalizations or idealist visions of reality could identify or portray. But how is human agency to be construed in its relation to the concepts of interest and power?

In order to answer this question, we have to understand Morgenthau's threefold conceptualization of the relations between power, interest, and morality (as discussed in "The Commitments of a Theory of International Relations", 1959; here 1962c, p. 59). *First,* morality can limit "the interests that power seeks and the means that power employs to that end"; *second*, "morality puts the stamp of its approval upon certain ends and means"; and, *third*, "morality serves interests and power as their ideological justification". In conclusion, Morgenthau argues that all manifestations of politics and their multiple empirical forms (as political institutions; systems of representation, decision-making, diplomacy, and negotiation; war and peace; international organizations; the international system of states; etc.), which are to be seen as expressions and creations of human agency, can best be made visible, cognizable, and studied through the heuristic application of the concepts of power, interest, and morality and their interrelation.

It is of great interest here to see (and correct) the confusion which Morgenthau's concepts of power, interest, and morality cause when taken as ontological statements rather than as epistemological concepts. A striking example, which tells us a complete story about Morgenthau being (wrongly) seen as defender and promoter of the nation-state, "its" *raison d'état*, and power politics, can be found in correspondence with Henry Kissinger during the 1950s. In 1949, Morgenthau published an article called "The Primacy of National Interest" in which he describes "national interest" as a further epistemological concept, criticizing all attempts to essentialize, reify, or define national interest, what it *is* or *what* it may consist of. He writes that national interest is "the standard of evaluation of foreign policies planned and pursued" (1949b, p. 208) and thus could operate as a critical device for reflecting upon foreign policy. National interest is hence not to be seen as some sort of statement on what the interest of the nation *is*, but rather as a synonym for critical reflection upon foreign policy. And this synonym is called "national interest" not for any substantive or substantializable reasons, but in opposition to universal moral standards according to his anti-idealist criticism and his warning of moral crusade(r)s.[12] In Morgenthau's work, national interest comprises and "solders" interest, power and morality into one concept; however, it does *not* do so in an ontological sense as *raison d'état* or in a claim for power politics, but as a historically contextualized epistemological concept and heuristic tool for the analysis of a distinct, contingent political environment, namely that of the 19th- and 20th-century world of nation-states and its fragmentation into particularistic actors.

Despite these very clear statements, this article contributed heavily to Morgenthau's (mis)reception as *Realpolitiker* by policy-makers and academic colleagues alike. Thence this paper became embraced last but not least by Henry Kissinger. As we know from many letters between Morgenthau and Kissinger during the 1950s, Morgenthau distanced himself from Kissinger's embracement, emphasizing his actual understanding of "national interest" and criticizing Kissinger for a lack of political judgment.[13] Morgenthau's opposition to his reception as advocate of realism as *Realpolitik* and its respective onto-logical assumptions is communicated further by his correspondence with Kindermann from the early 1960s regarding a German transla-tion of *Politics Among Nations*. We learn from respective letters, about Morgenthau's attempts to dispel all possibility that this book may be received as *Realpolitik* (as had occurred, for example, in a German review of *Politics Among Nations* by Werner Link). Morgenthau notes in a letter, dated April 5, 1961, regarding an imputed proximity between his book and Heinrich Treitschke:

> This is a complete misunderstanding of my position. Treitschke was the ideologue of the nation state ... and of power. I am an ana-lyst of the nation state and of power and have emphasized time and again their negative moral connotations. More particularly, I have emphasized the obsolesce of the nation state as a principle of political order.

Linking this back to the question of what Morgenthau's talk of politi-cal "facts" precisely means, we now see that all kinds of different polit-ical constellations and their spatio-temporally divergent forms, which become visible and possible to study through these threefold rela-tions between the concepts of power, interest, and morality are – and this represents the perennial "fact"(or) of politics – *created by human agency*.[14] This remains the same throughout human history in that men are "not simply a product of nature, but both the creature and creator of history and politics in and through which his/her individ-uality and freedom of choice manifest themselves"; in brief, humans are an Aristotelian "zoon politikon",[15] the creators of political order.

With regard to this perennial factor in politics, Morgenthau speaks, rather unfortunately, of a "law". Even if his actual writings are very concise and clear, he appears quite often to have used terminology, as in this case the term "law", which was prone to being misunderstood and which occasionally even sounded positivist.[16] Regarding his use of the word "law", we find, however, more clarification in his 1944 article "The Limitations of Science and the Problem of Social Planning" where, embedded in his criticism of rationalism, he writes that social laws are on a level which is not "the mythological level of absolute certainty and predictability, but that of statistical averages and probability" *at best*. And further:

> [T]he social scientist does not remain an indifferent observer but intervenes actively as both product and creator of social conditions...Thus it is in the quality of the human mind itself that the rationalistic analogy between physical and social world...finds its final refutation. Kepler and Newton, Grotius and the Abbe de St Pierre, and with them the Age of Reason were convinced that the rationality of nature corresponded to the rationality of the human mind and vice versa. (1944, p. 179)

In Morgenthau's philosophical commitment which sees humans being the creators of political order, and this "fact" being a perennial factor of politics, we have the only ontology in Morgenthau. This ontology consists of a political anthropology which construes humans as constituted by a natural desire for sociability (and love[17]) and power. Most revealing in this case is, further to his *The Concept of the Political*, a short article titled "Love and Power" (1962e) and his argument that both grow from the basic anthropological condition of *loneliness*. In his/her efforts and struggle to overcome loneliness, men will refer to three activities, or better, forms of agency – religion, love, and power – since the condition of loneliness is unbearable for humans. Religion, love and the desire for sociability and power in their role to transcend loneliness hence become the forces and faculties for creation of community and political order – and remain in this role as the creative, sometimes also destructive, but still perennial forces of politics. The modern mind, in its attempts to rationalize, measure, and fabricate human agency and politics, will have become blind to these perennial forces and their significance for human life and politics. Morgenthau writes:

> The inability of the modern mind to see this connection between love and power is the measure of its inability to see the true dimension of either love or power...transcending all historic

configurations, [and] antedating them...Of all creatures, only man is capable of loneliness because only he is in need of not being alone, without being able in the end to escape being alone. It is that striving to escape his loneliness which gives the impetus to both the lust for power and the longing for love, and it is the inability to escape that loneliness. (1962e, p. 247)

According to these views, power[18] appears not as ultimately and primarily a force for social and political domination, nor as a materialist and materializeable capacity; but rather as men's puissance and potency to act in order to transcend his/her own natural limitations.[19] In Morgenthau's lectures from the winter terms of 1949 and 1952 (see, for example, 1949a) we read the very instructive formulation of power as "a pluralism of antagonisms". Ultimately, the emphasis on power in Morgenthau and his philosophical commitment to the political anthropology of the human as creator and creature of politics is the attempt to bring humankind and the human factor back into politics. It is thus to be seen as intertwined with his criticism of rationalism, empiricism, and idealism and all attempts to rationalize, measure, and fabricate political order. As such, power itself is neither good nor bad; it can be both productive and destructive; what is more or less justified, thus possible to judge in a moral sense, are the *means* to accomplish and exert power.[20]

The question of objectivity

A third philosophical commitment resonating with Morgenthau's epistemology can be learned from the very first of his "Six Principles..." (1954), which contains another terminologically difficult, because so readily mistakable, sentence: "Political realism believes that politics, like society in general, is governed by objective laws that have their roots in human nature." What could open the door to mistaken positivist interpretation more than this, especially in an intellectual climate of American Political Science in the 1950s and 60s that was obsessed with finding objective social laws, their representation in theory, and the predictability of politics according to such laws? But when we contextualize this statement, we decipher a thoroughly hermeneutic position. Our attention must be placed here on Morgenthau's use of 'objective'/objectivity when he states that politics are governed by objective laws. It is helpful to consult here another quotation from the third of his "Six Principles..." (1963): "Realism assumes that its key concept of interest defined as power is an objective category which is universally valid, but it does not endow that concept with a meaning that is fixed once and for all."

As we can see here, objectivity does not refer to an eternal sameness of reality – that is, to a reality of never-changing characteristics which would be knowable and describable on the basis of ever-valid, truthful sentences; rather objectivity is understood by Morgenthau in the philosophical tradition of Nietzsche and neo-Kantians Max Weber and Heinrich Rickert as an analysis based upon explicitly formulated conceptual distinctions in order to perceive/find out/ identify/recognize/analyze features and qualities of an object in question; thus qualities which form part of the object studied and which reveal themselves from the object (i.e., *ex re*, emanating from the object/thing), becoming cognizable *only* by clear and elaborated concepts. This is a very different understanding of objectivity than the understanding promoted by positivist science and everyday language; it is an understanding of objectivity which Nietzsche describes as "our concept of this thing" which becomes increasingly complete the more "different eyes we can use to observe the thing" (1969, p. 19).[21] Finally, we see that Morgenthau describes "interest defined as power" as such a concept which would deliver an "objective [in the sense explained] category", as an epistemological concept, which was "universally valid", but only as an *epistemological tool* to perceive/find out/identify/recognize/analyze reality and *not* as an empirical statement about, or a representation of, reality.[22] This leads us directly to the fourth philosophical commitment of realist epistemology which can be summarized as the *"Standortgebundenheit"* of knowledge and theory.

"Standortgebundenheit" and relationality of knowledge and theory

There are several threads throughout his oeuvre where Morgenthau points out that all theory and theoretical analysis are contingent upon factors the occurrences of which we had no knowledge of and consequences which we could not foresee. Even if prominently communicated in *The Concept of the Political*, it was, to our knowledge, not before a talk at the University of Maryland in 1961, with the title "The Intellectual and Political Functions of a Theory of International Relations" (here 1962b), that Morgenthau used the precise term *"standortgebunden"* to describe the spatial and temporal conditionality of political and social theory and knowledge. The term *"standortgebunden"*, or *"Standortgebundenheit"*, is from sociologist Karl Mannheim and is a key concept of Mannheim's sociology of knowledge (1936; see also 1984). It describes the idea that social theory always depends upon the social and political environment in which it has been formulated and in which it is supposed to operate. This term endorses a *relationist* and *perspectivist* understanding of objectivity as discussed above in the sense of an object revealing characteristics of itself *in relation* to concepts and perspectives applied. Accordingly, all social and political being and respective knowledge are historical and spatial in their essence. In addition to his respective statements from *The Concept of the Political*, we find, in the third of Morgenthau's "Six Principles...", *no less than three paragraphs* which most explicitly explain this position in relation to the concepts of power and interest and therefore may be quoted here at some length:

[The] kind of interest determining political action in a particular period of history depends upon the political and cultural context within which foreign policy is formulated. The goals that might be pursued by nations in their foreign policy can run the whole gamut of objectives any nation has ever pursued or might possibly pursue...

The same observations apply to the concept of power. Its content and the manner of its use are determined by the political and cultural environment... Power covers all social relationships which serve that end, from physical violence to the most subtle psychological ties by which one mind controls another...

What is true of the general character of international relations is also true of the nation state as the ultimate point of reference of contemporary foreign policy... [The] contemporary connection between interest and the nation state is a product of history, and is therefore bound to disappear in the course of history. (Morgenthau, from the third of his "Six Principles...", 1963)

Morgenthau's epistemological position of *"Standortgebundenheit"* thus coincides with his criticism of the rationalist and positivist ideas of historical progress, techniques of social engineering and the rationality of the "Age of Reason" which all require a universal standpoint of knowledge from which to derive these ideas and respective strategies for their realization; a standpoint, which cannot exist according to the notion of *"Standortgebundenheit"*. Further to his published oeuvre – such as *Scientific Man vs Power Politics* (1946), "The State of Political Science" (here 1962a) or his *Concept of the Political* – from which we know these critiques, we have additional evidence from his 1949(a) lecture "Philosophy of International Relations" (very similar also from his 1952 lecture on the same topic), as well as most strikingly from letters between Morgenthau and Kindermann dating from the 1960s (see HJM-Archive Box 33).

An epistemic ethics of anti-hubris

Finally, we can conclude from these discussions the existence of an epistemologically based ethics of anti-hubris in Morgenthau's political theory. This ethics speaks out strongly against definitive knowledge claims about and representational reifications of the political *à la* Carl Schmitt or "neo"-"realism". This ethics is aware of the limits of the knowability of the political; it is careful about explaining causes of political occurrences; about presuming strict relations between cause and effects; about concluding predictions of political events; with essentialist statements regarding the nature/identity of events and actors (and as such it is "anti-foundationalist"); and finally about definite policy conclusions deduced from such claims and/or statements. Claiming knowledge of the political, which would allow all this, appears for Morgenthau as hubris. This is an important aspect of Morgenthau's understanding and conceptualization of the political: not only in his elaboration and emphasis of this epistemological commitment, but further in pointing to the idea (inherent most explicitly in his reference to Mannheim's concept of *"Standortgebundenheit"*) that theoretical explication, analysis, and understanding depend on spatio-historical constellations and their contingencies that bear upon *how* one frames the problems, concepts, and perspectives of analysis and the field in which interpretation is able even to take place. Consequently, the concept of the political in Morgenthau is *"standortgebunden"* itself, thus as historically contingent, ephemeral and transient as are, for example, his "Six Principles of Political Realism".[23] Nevertheless, his concept of the political establishes and provides a regime of knowledge (production) and critical analysis of (international) politics in the time of nation-states – and was intended to provide such a regime; not, however, in the way it became read, manipulated, and instrumentalized in the discipline of International Relations, but with the idea and hope of becoming superfluous itself due to Morgenthau's hope that the nation-state was itself also an ephemera.

4
Morgenthau's Twofold Concept of Power

The final aspect of Morgenthau's thought, which we want to discuss in this introduction, is his concept of power. Power has always been of major cognitive interest in the pursuit of analyzing Morgenthau's contribution to International Relations (e.g., Wasserman, 1959; Nobel, 1995; Williams, 2004; Molloy, 2004; Hacke, 2005; Neacsu, 2010). Given the vastness of interpretations, we might rightfully ask what can a translation of *La notion du politique* significantly contribute to the understanding of Morgenthau's concept of power. To give a bold answer: it is essential because a close study of this important concept of Morgenthau's thought and its genealogical development demonstrates that he meticulously distinguished between two concepts of power – an empirical and a normative concept – in his European works while ignoring this most important distinction in his English writings.

Morgenthau understood power (and it is of no relevance here if we speak of empirical or normative power) not in simplistic terms of material capabilities as we often find it in "neo-realism", but as a concept of "durchgehende[r] Geistigkeit" (constant intellectuality) (1930c, p. 43). Power was, for Morgenthau, a psychogenic condition which rested on inter-subjective relations. It could not be acquired through an endogenous accumulation of financial means and/or weaponry; rather power was for Morgenthau generally created through the interaction of people: as a result and quality of human action. The distinction he made in his European writings – as in *La notion du politique* – between *Macht* and *Kraft* (1930c, p. 9; 1934b, p. 33) and *pouvoir* and *puissance* (i.e., between "power" and "puissance", the later being understood as

47

the faculty and capability to act, to express oneself, and to be creative) rested, therefore, not on power being the means to some kind
of end, but on power being the end in itself. As we will see below in
greater detail, Morgenthau understood empirical power as the ability
to dominate others, whereas normative power implied the intention
to willfully act together to contribute to the creation of a life-world. In
Scientific Man vs Power Politics, Morgenthau put the distinction between
power more figuratively: "[m]an is the victim of political power by
necessity; he is a political master by aspiration" (1946, p. 153).

That Morgenthau's concept of power is still much contested
in International Relations – him being very often misread as a
machtpolitische power politician and his twofold conceptualization
being not yet fully realized, acknowledged, or appreciated in the disciplinary debates – is partly his own responsibility, as he did not
clearly distinguish between his empirical and normative concept of
power in his English writings (thus from 1937 on). We have no concrete evidence as to why Morgenthau did not define his concept of
power in his English writings as sharply as he did in his German and
French ones. One reason might be related to the unfavorable climate
towards Germany during and shortly after the Second World War,
which is certainly why Morgenthau attempted to separate himself
from his past, including from his intellectual legacies. As we know
from his former student, Richard Ned Lebow, "questions about his
German past were taboo" (2003, p. 219). A second reason was presumably the shift of interest from purely theoretical studies towards
works with a higher focus on contemporary policy issues (Guzzini,
1998, p. 24), such as "The Problem of German Reunification" (1960b)
or *Vietnam and the United States* (1965). Still, this does not settle the
question why Morgenthau did not attempt to improve the clarity
of his concepts after his emigration to the United States, especially
since he seemed to have realized this problem very clearly. To Michael
Oakeshott, Morgenthau wrote in 1948 that

> I can now see clearly that my attempts to make clear the distinc-
> tions between rationalism and rational inquiry, scientism and sci-
> ence, were in vain. I think I was fully aware of the importance and
> difficulty of these distinctions ... and it is now obvious to me that
> I have failed in the task to make my meaning clear. (HJM-Archive
> Box 44)

Fortunately, with the translation of *La notion du politique* we can leave aside this problem and rather attend to the disentanglement of Morgenthau's twofold concept of power. In order to pursue this intention, this final part of the introduction will first elaborate Morgenthau's localization of power in human nature, before both concepts – *pouvoir* and *puissance* – are addressed.

Power and human nature

To illustrate the relation Morgenthau saw between power and human nature we have to begin with the above-mentioned (unpublished) manuscript "Über die Herkunft des Politischen aus der Natur des Menschen" ("The Derivation of the Political from Human Nature") which Morgenthau wrote three years before *La notion du politique*. There, Morgenthau argued that humans are defined by basic drives as they succumb to "the impulse of life striving to keep alive, to prove oneself and to interact with others" (1930c, p. 5; translation by the authors). From this quotation we can extract Morgenthau's view of the two fundamental drives of human nature: the drive for self-preservation ("*Selbsterhaltungstrieb*") and the drive to prove oneself ("*Bewährungstrieb*") (Morgenthau, 1930c, p. 15).

As Robert Schuett (2007, p. 59) recently stressed, Morgenthau's elaboration of these two drives is congruent to Sigmund Freud's concepts of ego and sexual instinct. If we consider that this manuscript was written at the time when he was working in Sinzheimer's law office and held close intellectual relations to the Institute for Social Research in which psychoanalysis, personified by Fromm, was well received, the consideration of Freud in Morgenthau's elaboration of human nature becomes understandable. Freud noted that "I took as my starting-point a saying of...Schiller that 'hunger and love are what moves the world'" (1961, p. 117). In Morgenthau's reasoning we find an almost identical passage:

> If the striving for the preservation of one's life is caused by a deficiency, one is, figuratively speaking, a child of hunger. If one is striving to balance or avoid a lack of energy, then this striving to prove oneself is caused by a surplus of energy seeking release. This finds, again speaking figuratively, one of its most characteristic expressions in love. (1930c, pp. 5–6; translation by the authors)

Despite the fact that Morgenthau considered the drive for self-preservation (such as hunger) to be the more fundamental, as humans always attempt to first preserve their life, we can leave its elaboration aside as this drive is of minor importance for Morgenthau's understanding of politics and his concept of power. We can instead turn to the drive to prove oneself (love). This drive to prove oneself is important because, as Morgenthau noted "[t]he desire for power … concerns itself not with the individual's survival, but with his position among his fellows once his survival has been secured" (1946, p. 165). This demonstrates that we cannot understand Morgenthau's concept of power in a Hobbesian tradition as a means of self-preservation (Good, 1960, p. 612; Murray, 1996, p. 84; Frei, 2001, p. 127) – something for which Morgenthau has been, up to this day, unjustly criticized (e.g., Tucker, 1952; Ringmar, 1996, p. 50; Forndran, 1997, p. 47; Hall, 2006, p. 1161). And this despite the fact that he publicly repudiated this connection to Hobbes, as exemplified in a letter to the editors of *International Affairs* in which he criticized Martin Wight for having made this connection (Morgenthau, 1959c, p. 502). Two aspects of the drive to prove oneself deserve to be further elaborated as they influence his conceptualizations of power.

First, only when the drive to prove oneself touches upon other people does it become of political interest. For Morgenthau, generally the intention of this drive was to make oneself aware of one's own life and thereby establish an awareness of one's own strengths and capabilities. As this can only happen in relation to other people, this drive is manifested, for example, in the effect it has on gender relations, but also in games, and in artistic and academic expression. Hence, "everywhere the human being strives to show 'what he/she is capable of'" (Morgenthau, 1930c, p. 6; translation by the authors). We see, in fact, the manifestation of the drive to prove oneself at the origin of this striving. This strive is entirely directed towards gaining and increasing pleasure and, in particularly challenging situations, it promises the highest surplus in pleasure since such situations require overcoming obstacles by mastering non-routine circumstances (Morgenthau, 1930c, pp. 26–7). Only then can one's identity be assured through the appraisal of others and provide the aspired to surplus of pleasure (Morgenthau, 1930c, pp. 31–2). However, only when in these interpersonal relationships the drive to prove oneself takes an explicit interest in humans does it become of an explicitly political nature, as the following quotation from *Science: Servant or Master?* demonstrates:

> Thus the scholar seeking knowledge seeks power; so does the poet who endeavors to express his thoughts and feelings in words. So do the mountain climber, the hunter, the collector of rare objects. They all seek to assert themselves as individuals against the world by mastering it. It is only when they choose as their object other men that they enter the political sphere. (1972, p. 31)

Second, human existence was for Morgenthau characterized by tragedy. This stems partly from this drive to prove oneself, because it is excessive. Neither the potential gain of pleasure nor the objects to which it can be directed know any limit (Morgenthau, 1930c, p. 70). In his doctoral thesis, Morgenthau remarked that any and all questions can become interesting for this drive since they "are seized at random, irrespective of the actual content" (1929, pp. 126–7; translation by the authors). Therefore, satisfaction of one's pleasure can be aspired to, but, due to its limitlessness, never achieved. Only a few times has the pleasure principle nearly reached its achievement, for which, to symbolize, Morgenthau (1945b, p. 13; 1946, p. 166) chose the love of Don Juan and Faust's thirst for knowledge. More than 15 years earlier, Morgenthau (1930c, p. 71) also included in this list the imperial aspirations of Alexander the Great and Napoleon Bonaparte. However, these were exceptions and their aspiring also failed since *vanitas* (transience) took hold of Don Juan, Faust, and Alexander, and the current of the Berezina washed away Napoleon's ambitions. A further tragedy reflected in the drive to prove oneself was, according to Morgenthau (1930c, pp. 75–7) and Freud (1961, p. 117), that its extreme limitlessness enters into conflict with the drive for self-preservation and could eventually mean one's life was endangered as well as the lives of others.

Locating power in human nature by characterizing it as a constant urge to ideational self-realization in interpersonal relationships allowed Morgenthau to turn away from ontological considerations and towards a distinction of power in terms of its social utilization. For Morgenthau, as soon as people interact power is created. The attempt to eradicate power is, therefore, pointless; rather the focus should be on *what kind of power* is established. As we will now see, Morgenthau argued that power in its empirical form (*pouvoir*) allows for the de-politicization of social life as politics is reduced to an institutionalized understanding, whereas power in its normative form (*puissance*) establishes the political as it enables people to pursue their interests and act together for the common good.

Pouvoir: the empirical concept of power

In modern societies, Morgenthau argued, power, evoked through the drive to prove oneself, was predominantly empirically traceable in the form of the *animus dominandi*, "the desire for power" (1946, p. 165), which literally means the lust for *domination* among people. As shown in Morgenthau's statement, "je constate simplement ce que je vois" (1936, p. 5), he was aware of the necessity to deal with this concept *analytically* as socio-political developments in modern societies had reduced power to a tool of domination.

Modern societies had voided people of their metaphysical foundation. The de-humanizing effects of this void were of much concern for the early Morgenthau, as the content of numerous unpublished manuscripts suggest. Ranging from "Suicide with a Good Conscience" (1930b) to "Über den Sinn der Wissenschaft in dieser Zeit und über die Bestimmung des Menschen" ("On the Meaning of Scholarship in Our Time") (1934b) and "Kann in unserer Zeit eine objektive Moralordnung aufgestellt werden? Wenn ja, worauf kann sie gegründet werden? Kennwort: Metaphysik" ("Can an Objective Moral Order be established in Our Time?") (1937), Morgenthau elaborated on the reasons and effects of this development. Indeed, even in *Science: Servant or Master?* (1972), one of his latest major intellectual contributions, Morgenthau returned to this concern as he acknowledged in its preface that part of this book rested on the manuscript from 1934. Beginning with the Enlightenment in the second half of the 18th century, absolutistic power-structures and the cultural dominance of Christianity was broken up by the Age of Reason. Reason allowed one to gain a sober outlook on the world through the rigorous application of scientific methods and eventually promised a self-determined life as people realized that they were responsible for their own life and not born into a religiously informed supernatural social structure. However, Erik Ringmar (2006) informs us that to this seemingly liberating movement, there was also a darker side. Reason not only had the power to liberate, but also to create restraints as it fostered increasing industrialization (*Hochindustrialisierung*) in the 19th century (Osterhammel, 2009, pp. 102–3). In the industrialized societies of Europe traditional social structures and personal living conditions deteriorated in an urbanized environment while technological advancements subordinated the self-determined use of time to the meticulous observance of shift work and timetables. Eventually, this constant accountability, measurement and justification to others, as well as the subjection to efficiency, created a 'poor social environment' (Ringmar, 2006, p. 918). People yearned to break free from this 'directionless, frantic change' (Rosa, 2009, p. 102) in which the Age of Reason had put them. This is why, according to Ringmar, the 19th century was also a "century of dreams" as Romanticism, naturalist movements, and the fascination which the exotic (exemplified in chinoiserie and orientalism) prospered. In addition, for the same reason, the 19th century also saw the rise of ideologies.

Ideologies had gained momentum in the 19th century, with nationalism, liberalism, conservatism, and socialism, and climaxed in the early 20th century with fascism and communism. The rise of ideologies concerned Morgenthau as they restricted human drives and deprived people of their capacities. Nationalism was particularly at the centre of Morgenthau's attention as the principle of sovereignty provided nation-states with the means to enforce homogeneity domestically through the institutionalization of education, a reinterpretation of history and the standardization of language (Snyder, 2011, p. 58). The developments leading to the creation of the German Empire in 1871 are a case in point, which we want to consider before we further elaborate Morgenthau's specific concern about ideologies. The transformation of the hostile "system of ministates" (Hobsbawm, 1990, p. 31) of the Holy Roman Empire of the German Nation (*Imperium Romanum Sacrum Nationis Germanicæ*) into the "belated nation" (Helmuth Plessner) was achieved through a rigorous national homogenization. Already in 1812 Prussia had introduced the *Abitur* as the official entry requirement for institutions of higher education, and this was swiftly followed by other German states, becoming the standard in 1834 (Ringer, 1969, pp. 16–32). This standardization of education allowed the state to control knowledge transfer through a common curriculum and create an obedient bureaucracy (Vierhaus, 1972, pp. 523–5). Equally, as the rise of historicism[1] demonstrates, history was reinterpreted as a teleological process that had received its climax with the unification of the German states in the Hall of Mirrors of the Palace of Versailles in 1871. To ensure that this interpretation of history did not remain solely an academic discourse, its visualization for the entire public was achieved through the construction of monuments throughout Germany exemplified in the *Hermannsdenkmal* in the Teutoburg Forest, the *Kyffhäuser Monument* in central Germany, or the *Völkerschlachtsdenkmal* in Leipzig.[2] This ideologization of life concerned Morgenthau (1960b) as it deprived humans of the right to establish and pursue their interests in two ways.

First, ideologies promote creative mediocrity. Humans are not able to fully utilize all their creative abilities within an ideological framework such as the nation-state. Ideologies are established to create a discourse of legitimacy for the current political order, but they also provide "ontological security" (Giddens, 1984, p. 375; see also endnote 5). Retaining the social structures is, therefore, a vital expression of this legitimacy and security. An alteration of these structures through the creative abilities of humans ultimately means that people are threatened with losing their ontological security due to changes to the reification of their thought. Consequently, the creative abilities of humans are only used to support the ideologized reality by constraining them into a bureaucratic order. Second, ideologies also promote intellectual mediocrity. This was the case because conflicting worldviews or merely a critical potential challenges the political order and cannot be tolerated. Anyone who questions these narratives through his/her beliefs, knowledge, or even existence has to be excluded. This exclusion may range from criminalization to expulsion and even extinction, as happened in fascism and communism. Morgenthau (1984, pp. 363–4) was confronted with the consequences of otherness during the earlier-mentioned soirée in Munich in 1935, to which he had been invited by the jurist Neumeyer, when the other guests remained largely indifferent to the execution of a befriended Jewish lawyer.

For Morgenthau, in this ideologized environment, the drive to prove oneself had to exhaust itself in the form of the *animus dominandi*. Morgenthau's use of terminology reveals that this empirical concept of power rested on Weber's well-known definition of power.

He defined power as "the probability that one actor within a social relationship will be in a position to carry out his own will despite resistance, regardless of the basis on which this probability rests" (Weber, 1978, p. 53). Indeed, in *Politics Among Nations* we find a similar definition by Morgenthau. He remarked that "[p]olitical power is a psychological relation between those who exercise it and those over whom it is exercised. It gives the former control over certain actions of the latter through the impact which the former exerts on the latter's minds" (1985, p. 32). However, reducing power to a lust for domination meant that interpersonal relationships were conflict-driven and the potential for aggression was constantly looming over the heads of people. To hinder the outbreak of violence domestically, nation-states had to erect moral, societal, and/or legal restraints the assertiveness of which Morgenthau elaborated in his post-doctoral thesis *La réalité des normes* (1934a). Without restraints the existence of nation-states would otherwise be threatened as we also read in Freud:

> The existence of this tendency to aggression...is the factor that disturbs our relation with our neighbors and makes it necessary for culture to institute its high demands. Civilized society is perpetually menaced with disintegration through this...hostility of men towards one another...Culture has to call up every possible reinforcement in order to erect barriers against the aggressive instincts of men. (1953, pp. 37–8)

Yet, as Morgenthau argued in his doctoral (1929) and postdoctoral thesis (1934a), on the international level, there would be no such restrictions – at best only moral ones – to hinder people from seeking to fulfill their lust for domination. Indeed, nation-states, as Morgenthau (1930b) had argued since the beginning of his career, ruthlessly employed "cultural blinders" (2004, p. 36) which encouraged people to pursue their lust for domination on the international level. The two world wars and the *Shoah* (holocaust) were powerful personal experiences for Morgenthau which demonstrated the devastation this lust could cause. Through identification with the nation-state especially at times of crisis, by "rallying around the flag", to use a more modern term, each person could satisfy his/her lust by receiving a share of the power a nation acquires on the international scene (Schuett, 2007, pp. 61–6; Scheuerman, 2009, pp. 37–8).

From Weber, Morgenthau also borrowed the consequences, particularly on the international level, that this conceptualization of power entails. In *Politics as Vocation*, which Morgenthau read enthusiastically (Shilliam, 2007, p. 312), Weber noted that "[w]hen we say that a question is 'political'…we always mean the same thing. This is that the interests involved in the distribution or preservation of power, or a shift in power, play a decisive role in resolving that question" (2004, p. 33). Frei (2001, p. 130) has remarked that Morgenthau already referred to these strategies in his doctoral thesis (1929, p. 59), but only in *La notion du politique* did he become explicit. Power "peut viser à maintenir la puissance acquise, à l'augmenter ou à la manifester" (Morgenthau, 1933, p. 43): due to human nature, the aspiration for power, in the sense of the lust for domination, would require one to maintain, increase, and eventually demonstrate one's power. This intellectual congruence of Morgenthau to Weber in the understanding of empirical power led numerous International Relations scholars to comment on Morgenthau as an apologist of power politics (e.g., Pichler, 1998; Barkawi, 1998; Turner, 2009; Turner and Mazur, 2009). Indeed, almost 15 years later, Morgenthau used exactly the same outline in *Politics Among Nations* noting that "[a]ll politics…reveals three basic patterns…either to keep power, to increase power, or to demonstrate power" (1985, p. 52) and in this textbook he went on to meticulously analyze the different forms of empirical power.

Yet, *Politics Among Nations* cannot be read as a theory, let alone a grand theory, of international politics as the subtitle of the German edition (Morgenthau, 1963) as well as International Relations mainstream perceptions made the reader believe; rather we have recently argued that Morgenthau's thought itself has to be seen as spatially and temporally conditioned, hence as "historically and politically contingent" (Behr, 2010, p. 215). This means, if we look more closely at *Politics Among Nations*, that Morgenthau's intention was to write a counter-ideology to nationalism and fascism as he acknowledged in the preface. Therefore, the concept of power he presented there was understood by Morgenthau as the empirically dominant version in an ideologized world, but equally we see that he was fundamentally opposed to such an understanding of power which reduced power to an unhindered lust for domination. In the above-mentioned letter to Oakeshott, written shortly after the publication of the first edition of

Politics Among Nations, Morgenthau argued that this ideologization had reduced the creative abilities of humans because they were intellectually unaware of their capacity to create their life-world, which is why "[m]an is tragic because he cannot do what he ought to do" (HJM-Archive Box 44). This explains why Morgenthau was initially reluctant to reissue *Politics Among Nations* as the correspondence between Morgenthau and his publisher Alfred A. Knopf was drawn out over several months (HJM-Archive Box 121). Yet, we see that the escalating Cold War convinced Morgenthau that the age of ideologies was far from over and *Politics Among Nations* had yet to serve its purpose as he repeated the assessment he had given Oakeshott in a letter to Richard S. Cohen of October 4, 1962 (HJM-Archive Box 10).

Puissance: the normative concept of power

Normatively, however, Morgenthau aspired to a different kind of power than *pouvoir* that prevailed in the ideologized world of the early and mid-20th century. This is the case because "[t]o say that a political action has no moral purpose is absurd" as "political action can be defined as an attempt to realize moral values through the medium of politics, that is, power" (1962d, p. 110). *Puissance*, the form of power he argued ought to be the defining factor in politics, is not characterized by domination; rather people are empowered to act together through the alignment of their antagonism of interests in order to create their life-world in self-determination. In short, whereas *pouvoir* is ultimately a negative concept, Morgenthau achieved with *puissance* a positive definition of power.

To arrive at such a positive concept, which is nothing less than an expression of Morgenthau's deep-rooted humanism or what Arendt would have called *amor mundi* (Young-Bruehl, 1982, p. 324), Morgenthau began his intellectual journey with Nietzsche's *amor fati* (2003, p. 157). In order to love the world, people had at first to embrace their destiny. This destiny is the initial recognition of Nietzsche's eternal recurrence. In *Thus spoke Zarathustra* Nietzsche noted that "[e]verything goes, everything returns; the wheel of existence rolls forever. Everything dies, everything blossoms anew; the year of existence runs on forever... Everything departs, everything meets again; the ring of existence is true to itself forever" (1969, p. 234). Just like Walter Benjamin's notion of "homogeneous, empty time" (1999,

p. 252), Nietzsche employed a nihilistic concept of time and space that contradicted any teleological life-stories. Understanding this initial aimlessness and meaninglessness, Morgenthau was convinced that people would realize that, in modern societies, ideologization had deprived them of their capacity to construct their own life-world and make use of all their abilities.

Yet, Morgenthau was also aware that this nihilism is, at least in the beginning, a great disappointment to humans since it "offers with each answer new questions, with each victory a new disappointment, and thus seems to lead nowhere. In this labyrinth of unconnected causal connections man discovers many little answers but no answer to the great questions of his life, no meaning, no direction" (1946, p. 176). Countless combinations of actions and reactions provide a myriad of ever-recurrent moments which evolve without pre-pre-scribed purpose or aim. However, Nietzsche's concept does not imply surrendering to nihilism, but overcoming it. In a later work, which remained unpublished during his lifetime, Nietzsche accentuated that "[t]he unalterable sequence of certain phenomena demonstrates no 'law' but a power relationship between two or more forces" (1968, p. 336). This means that these returning moments should not solely be agonized over, but that one can choose to affirm and endorse them. This is the *amor fati*, the embracing of one's destiny, because endorsing such recurrences means relating these initially meaning-less moments to oneself; and, thereby, by even altering them ever so slightly, transforming them into significant situations. This positive attribution enables people to overcome their surrounding nihilism since, as Lee Spinks mentions, they recognize that "life is an eternal movement of becoming" (2003, p. 131).

However, accepting the *amor fati* is not only disappointing: it also primarily denotes a dolorous affair since it causes, in György Lukács's words, a "transcendental homelessness" (1963, p. 41). Rather, people yearn for the transcendental shelter of ideologies' ontological security. This shelter is provided by a carefree (at least to a certain extent), clearly structured life as conceptions of rea-son, virtue, justice, and even pity or happiness are standardized. The price to be paid for this ontological security by, in Nietzsche's words, "the ultimate man" (*letzter Mensch*) (1969, p. 45) is the renun-ciation of one's subjectivity. However, once, people accept their fate they can become an *Übermensch*. This Nietzschean concept has long suffered from obscure racist interpretations and only recently has scholarship started to excavate the importance of this concept for Morgenthau's concept of power (Neacsu, 2010, p. 99). With the *Übermensch*, Morgenthau was provided with an ideal-type for what it takes to arrive at a positive connotation of power. It is the recognition of eternal recurrence and at the same time the renunciation of an ideologized life through encyclopedic knowledge, the ability to intellectually alienate oneself from one's life-world and thereby recognize that knowledge-construction is temporally and spatially conditioned. These are qualities, as we know from the above-quoted review of Morgenthau's *The Purpose of American Politics*, which Morgenthau himself endorsed. The *Übermensch* is provided with the ability to recognize *and* the will to overcome the surrounding nihilistic world. Through self-restraint, self-assurance, and particularly self-reflection, he/she is able to refer the ever-recurrent moments to him/herself and, thereby, create meaning and eventually identity, as Morgenthau argued in congruence with Nietzsche. *Puissance* was for Morgenthau, therefore, also the self-capability to create identity because it is not achieved through the distinction from "otherness", but in togetherness through one's own will. As Ringmar has put it:

> [w]hat we must do is...to *create* a present for our selves; we must *make room* for our selves in time and space. This is the task which a constitutive story fulfills by extending our being in space and in time. It is with the construction of a constitutive story that our selves come to exist, and it is with the destruction of a constitutive story that our selves disappear. (1996, p. 76; emphasis in the original)

It is particularly for this reason that Morgenthau deplored the absence of the qualities of an *Übermensch* in *Science: Servant or Master?*:

> [t]his meaningless and aimless activity may convey the superficial appearance of an abundant dynamism trying to transform the empirical world. In truth, however, it is not the pressure of creative force but flight from his true task that drives man beyond himself through action. In the intoxication of incessant activity, man tries to forget the question posed by the metaphysical shock.

Yet, since the noise of the active world can drown out that question but cannot altogether silence it, complete oblivion, which is coincident with the end of consciousness itself, becomes the unacknowledged ultimate aim. (1972, pp. 48–9)

Achieving the stage of an *Übermensch* by being able to create one's own identity leads eventually to total liberation since "[w]illing liberates: that is the true doctrine of will and freedom" (Nietzsche, 1969, p. 111). It liberates people from the reactionary forces of ideologies that control constructions of life-worlds in order to affirm the *status quo*. The *Übermensch* also liberates from ostensible eternal dichotomies. This is the case because these dichotomies do not have universal meaning, but are created to legitimize cultural habits and policies (Nietzsche, 1969, pp. 84–6). Morgenthau's refusal of such ostensibly absolute, yet simplifying dichotomies is stipulated in a letter to Bryon Dobell, then editor of *Book World*, from the 9 July 1968, which deserves to be quoted at length due to its forceful charge of the de-politicization of modern societies:

[N]ot being God, I am unable to pass judgment on student dissent in terms of "good" or "bad". What the students revolt against in the universities is what they are revolting against in the world at large. That world, thoroughly secularized and dedicated to the production of consumer goods and weapons of mass destruction, has lost its meaning. The university does not raise, let alone answer, the existential questions the students ask about themselves and their world. That world is also thoroughly mechanized and bureaucratized. Thus it diminishes the individual who must rely on others rather than himself for the satisfaction of his wants, from the necessities of life to his spiritual and philosophical longings. (HJM-Archive Box 43)

From this quotation, the scholar of International Relations can infer that politics was for Morgenthau a social realm in which people would not have to succumb to structural obligations manifested in dichotomies of good and bad, right and wrong, or friend and foe, as Schmitt had argued and for which he was criticized by Morgenthau, but that *puissance* enabled people to follow their interests and participate in the creation of their own life-world.

A further example, at first glance peculiar, yet in its peculiarity very forceful, will additionally stress Morgenthau's insistence on liberation through meaning-attribution: this is the example of death. Questions of death concerned Morgenthau from the very beginning of his academic career and we find references to it throughout his oeuvre, ranging from the early manuscript *Suicide with a Good Conscience* (1930b) to his late work *Science: Servant or Master?* (1972). It is in this latter study that the student of Morgenthau's work can understand that death was a form of liberation for him. Certainly, death "is the very negation of all man's experiences as specifically human in his existence: the consciousness of himself and of his world, the remembrance of things past and the ambitions of things to come, a creativeness in thought and action that aspires to ... the eternal" (Morgenthau, 1972, p. 144). Still, Morgenthau argued that even for humans who disapproved of religious discourses of eternity or ideological promises of immortality, death would signify no end of liberation. He saw one explanation in the pieces of reminiscence which people leave behind as a result of their efforts to actively give meaning to life. Furthermore, even death itself can become a liberating experience since, by committing suicide with a good conscience, people are enabled to master their biological death by choosing the place, time, and even tenor of their own death (Morgenthau, 1972, pp. 144–5).

To sum up so far, on his way to establishing a positive connotation of power Morgenthau again relied primarily on his *"Jugendliebe"* (early love) (Frei, 1994, p. 102): Nietzsche. It was he who showed Morgenthau that the will to power rested on the ability to discern. To be able to understand nihilism and to overcome it by attaching value to initially insignificant moments, hence, by relating one's surrounding world to oneself, the will to power finds its expression. Nietzsche remarked that "[m]an first implanted values into things to maintain himself – he created the meaning of things, a human meaning ... Only through evaluation is there value: and without evaluation the nut of existence would be hollow" (1969, p. 85). As the following translation of *La notion du "politique"* will demonstrate, Morgenthau picked up this "facteur psychologique, la volonté de puissance" (1933, p. 43) already in the 1930s and, even as late as the 1970s, he acknowledged that being a *homo faber* rather than an *animal laborans* enables the human to imbed "his biological existence within technological and social artefacts that survive that existence. His imagination creates new worlds of religion, art, and reason that live after their creator" (1972, p. 146).

As Morgenthau's terminology in *Science: Servant or Master?* indicates, for the last leg of his elaboration of *puissance* Morgenthau is to be seen in congruence with Arendt. He departed from Nietzsche as he had realized that Nietzsche's will to power accentuated the individual, but ignored social relations *and* more importantly did not provide answers to what *kind* of sociation these relations constructed. This critique was brought forward by Simmel (1995, pp. 361–2) in his study on Nietzsche and Arthur Schopenhauer, a work Morgenthau was well acquainted with (Frei, 2001, p. 100). Morgenthau repeated this critique in his manuscript on metaphysics, where he expressed concern about Nietzsche's promotion of the will to power for its own sake. Morgenthau did not endorse Nietzsche's view of a pre-existing reality which considered the will to power and its achievement as the highest ethical value in itself. On the contrary, the will to power had to be implemented for the achievement of a common good since "there is nothing more senseless for the human conscience than a morality which is indifferent to the dissolution of human society" (Morgenthau, 1937, p. 88; translation by the authors).

Contrastingly, the "thinking partnership" (Young-Bruehl, 1982, p. XV) between Morgenthau and Arendt offered Morgenthau the opportunity to consider the effects of power on a society at large. Interestingly, this crucial intellectual relationship is yet to be explored by International Relations scholarship if we neglect Christoph Rohde (2004, p. 98) who *en passant* refers to this thinking partnership without considering it further. Arendt and Morgenthau, who got to know each other in the 1950s while occasionally having lunch together at the University of Chicago faculty club, intensified their friendship during the 1960s when Arendt was also briefly teaching at the University of Chicago, due to their common disapproval of the Vietnam War; a friendship which culminated in an affectionate obituary from Morgenthau on the occasion of Arendt's death (Morgenthau, 1976; Young-Bruehl, 1982, pp. 383–9). Due to this close intellectual congruence, we can turn to Arendt's study *On Violence* from 1970, for which Morgenthau sent her affirmative remarks after the study received disapproving reviews (Young-Bruehl, 1982, pp. 424–5), as Morgenthau never elaborated his normative concept of power as concisely as Arendt. As the late publication date of Arendt's study shows, we are not arguing that Morgenthau may have copied Arendt's concept, or *vice versa*, but rather as the term "thinking partnership" indicates, that both were intellectually rooted in continental European humanities and that this intellectual background in combination with their academic and personal exchange fostered a similar understanding of power.

For Arendt "[p]ower corresponds to the human ability not just to act but act in concert. Power is never the property of an individual; it belongs to a group and remains in existence only so long as the group keeps together" (1970, p. 44). Hence, power signifies the consent of people to temporarily come together in a collective of speech and action by creating institutions, laws, and norms (Arendt, 1970, p. 41). Power was for Arendt (1970, p. 51), just as for Morgenthau (1929, p. 74; 1933, p. 43), not a means, but an end in itself which explains that both scholars, in agreement with Weber, distinguished between power and violence. Power is an end since only through its achievement is it possible to create a good life for humans in a society (Morgenthau, 2004, p. 30). The good life which is directed towards acquiring a common good (*bonum commune*) "is a life that is led by justice, which is also indicated by the general conception of politics ... that the philosophy of politics is really a subdivision of ethics" (Morgenthau, 2004, p. 56). In a letter to Edward Dew dated August 22, 1958, Morgenthau became a bit more explicit regarding what he meant by a good life. This was "the preservation of life and freedom in the sense of the Judeo-Christian tradition and ... of Kantian philosophy" (HJM-Archive Box 17). In a lecture on human rights about 20 years later, Morgenthau (1979, p. 25) largely repeated this definition. Certainly, it is legitimate to criticize Morgenthau for not further investigating the *kind* of sociation. Yet, this absence of a clearer definition of or investigation into the good life in Morgenthau's work demonstrates that it was a flexible concept for him in which the particular content is based on a consensus of interests of the people involved. The integrity and dignity of human life were considered by Morgenthau as its basic elements. It is especially the task of political leaders to have such a broad *telos* in mind since communities are led by them towards the achievement of the *bonum commune* (Morgenthau, 2004, p. 106). As Morgenthau noted in one of his lectures on Aristotle "[t]he virtue of a good ruler is identical with a good man. Because the good ruler, having to preside over a human society of which all human beings are members, must promote...the telos of man as such" (2004, p. 91). Power, then, became for Morgenthau a collective affair which enabled people to strive for the constant construction of their life-world by forming societies as temporal manifestations of the common good they could achieve through the alignment of their antagonism of interests. It is this willful construction of the life-world that makes Morgenthau's concept of power an expression of his *amor mundi*.

Notes

1   Overview of Morgenthau's Oeuvre and Worldview

1. We provide here, and in the following, English translations for originally German and French titles.
2. Further discussions of Morgenthau's notion of "objectivity" see Chapter 3 of this Introduction under "Morgenthau's Epistemological Commitments".

2   Contextualization of "The Concept of the Political"

1. Earlier attempts by Morgenthau to engage the question of the political resulted in two unpublished manuscripts – "Der Selbstmord mit gutem Gewissen" ("Suicide with a Good Conscience") (Morgenthau, 1930b) and "Über die Herkunft des Politischen aus dem Wesen des Menschen" ("The Derivation of the Political from Human Nature") (Morgenthau, 1930c).
2. The English translation of Morgenthau's lecture from German, which we suggest here, needs some explanation. The formulation in the German title *"Der Kampf...um die Realitaet des Staates"* implies two dimensions which could be presented in English as "The struggle...about the concept *and* reality of the state". On the one hand, Morgenthau has in mind the struggle of academia, primarily of *"deutsche Staatslehre"* [which has the same meaning as "Staatsrechtslehre"], regarding the concept of the state; on the other hand, such a concept has, as he argues, great influence on the political reality (*"Wirklichkeit"*) of the state. Thus, both the *concept* and the *reality* of the state are interlinked and expressed in the German formulation *"Der Kampf...um die Realitaet des Staates"*.
3. This reference is to be found in endnote 26 in Morgenthau's *Concept of the Political* (see Part II below) and refers to §324 of Hegel's Philosophy of Rights (*"Grundlinien der Philosophie des Rechts"*).
4. For Morgenthau's understanding of "objectivity" see below in Chapter 3 of this Introduction under "Morgenthau's Epistemological Commitments".
5. In relation to Morgenthau's criticism of *a priori* categories, see our discussions in Chapter 3 of this Introduction under "Morgenthau's Epistemological Commitments".
6. See also the discussion of the reification problem in Behr, 2010, Part IV.
7. See hereto the excellent reflections in Hoeber-Rudolph (2005) under the title of "The imperialism of categories: situating knowledge in a globalizing world" as well as the discussions in Behr/Rösch, 2010.
8. See hereto the discussions in Vollrath, 1987.

9. See below in Part II.
10. As Morgenthau noted in a lecture in 1942; see below in Chapter 3 of this Introduction under the heading "Morgenthau's Epistemological Commitments".
11. See more on this below in Chapter 3 of this Introduction under the heading "Morgenthau's Epistemological Commitments".
12. Such an edition ultimately failed and never came together because no German publisher would commit to such a publication.
13. Translation by the authors from a letter in which Morgenthau noted this suggested sub-chapter headline in German as *"Realismus als Revolte gegen den historischen Optimismus"*; see HJM-Archive Box 33.
14. See Chapter 3 of this Introduction under the heading "Morgenthau's Epistemological Commitments".
15. We very deliberately do not want to list names here as representatives of post-structuralism because this kind of labeling would contradict post-structuralist understanding of academia and of itself as basically an intellectual *movement*. Of course, however, there exist here the same dynamics as in academia and as in all disciplines in general, namely that some authors are more, and others less, referenced, and thus the emergence of proprietary tenets and disciplinary narratives occurs. As shall be the case with regard to classical realism and critical theory, our discussion does not claim completeness, but rather elaborates the main threads as they seem important for our contextualization indicatively focusing on some (i.e., focusing on some authors whose writings, or even single formulations, are seen as most indicative) while necessarily neglecting others. This neglect does not, however, imply statements about their relevance, but only about the indicativity of their problematizations and formulations for our discussions here.
16. In Chapters 3 and 4 of this Introduction under the headings "Morgenthau's Epistemological Commitments" and "Morgenthau's Twofold Concept of Power".
17. This formulation, of course, resembles Hannah Arendt's famous title from 1958 (see more below). This is quite deliberate. Arendt's and Morgenthau's work and their lives are interconnected in several aspects: they were colleagues for many years at the University of Chicago and later at the New School in New York; they shared the fate and experiences of Jewish scholar émigré; and they exchanged some 40 years of intense correspondence. What their post-emigration oeuvres seem to have in common, and what they share with many scholar émigrés of their generation is, as argued here, their common concern to bring humans and the human factor back into politics – even if this found very different articulations – which were perceived as excluded by positivist ideas of social planning, economic rationalizations, and individualistically fragmented interest-politics and related methodologies of American behavioralism.
18. In whose writings the return and the claim to bring back the political into a de-politicized, because bureaucratized and rationalized public sphere, is expressed maybe most explicitly by her writing with the same title (1999).

19. See more explicit comments on Morgenthau's arguments below in Chapter 4 of this Introduction under our discussion of his concept of power.

20. See this argument developed originally in their *Dialektik der Aufklärung* (1981, pp. 61–99).

21. In the following parts of this Introduction, see further discussions of the motif of *hubris* below at the end of Chapter 3 "Morgenthau's Epistemological Commitments"; of his criticism of idealist epistemology and idealism in politics also see Chapter 3; and of this "tragic vision of politics" in our discussions of the concept of power in Morgenthau below in Chapter 3 under "The human condition of politics" and in Chapter 4 "Morgenthau's Twofold Concept of Power".

22. See hereto Aristotle (2009), *Nichomachean Ethics*, Book 6.

23. See hereto more below in Chapter 4 under the heading "Morgenthau's Twofold Concept of Power", "Puissance: the normative concept of power".

24. In Chapter 1 of this Introduction "Overview of Morgenthau's Oeuvre and Worldview".

25. The reading and interpretation of intellectual traditions and legacies by Jim George seems to be in this regard outstandingly redundant and superficial (see, for example, 1994).

26. Further to our discussions here, see, among others, Behr (2010, especially Part IV) and the literatures discussed here.

27. See more on this below under Chapter 3 "Morgenthau's Epistemological Commitments", especially under "The question of objectivity" and "'Standortgebundenheit' and relationality of knowledge and theory".

3   Morgenthau's Epistemological Commitments

1. What follows here is a seriously abbreviated discussion, using simplifying labels, but bearing in mind that the views of individual philosophies and epistemologies labeled are indeed more subtle and complex than each classification suggests. However, the following discussion is useful when centering the key epistemological question around the *problématique* of which status is assigned to external worlds in terms of their mind-dependence or mind-independence.

2. From his *Discours de la methode* (1996); see also "Descartes' Epistemology" (2005); similar epistemological positions can be assigned to Spinoza and Leibniz (see "Rationalism vs Empiricism", 2008).

3. We use the term "epistemological security", similar to Anthony Giddens's term "ontological security" (1984, p. 375), as people's longing for the solidity and trustworthiness of their worldview and the guarantee of this solidity through social structures. Correspondingly, "epistemological security" would be a state of sureness and certainty in our knowledge about the world and the knowability of such worldviews.

4. See, for this fundamental realist epistemological position, Feldmann (1999) on "Contextualism and Skepticism" who writes: "The application

of the general idea of context dependence to knowledge attributions is straightforward. What it takes for a knowledge ... to be true can vary from context to context" (p. 93); also Feldmann (2001) and DeRose (2009).

5. See Nietzsche (1990), *On the Advantages and Disadvantages of History for Life*. Hereto, also interesting, is Emmanuel Lévinas's argument that the "purely empirical is that which received signification, not that gives it" in his paper "Meaning and Sense" (1996, p. 38).

6. Morgenthau used the metaphor of a "map" frequently: see 1955, 1959a, 1959b, 1971.

7. See here also Turner and Mazur (2009, p. 492): "The centrality of power and interest is not derived directly from the facts of international politics ... Power and interest are made central by the standpoint around which we have chosen to organize our inquiries." In their interesting and in many parts agreeable paper, Stephen Turner and George Mazur commit, however, the same error which they otherwise criticize: namely to single out one author as *the* influential figure for Morgenthau despite a lack of textual evidence in Morgenthau's writings themselves. In their case it is Max Weber. We could also mention William Scheuerman, who singles out Carl Schmitt, or Christoph Frei, who identifies Nietzsche. On the other hand, it is hard to understand why Turner and Mazur, while looking for these kinds of influences on Morgenthau, neglect Karl Mannheim even though his influence is most obvious when Morgenthau adopts and endorses Mannheim's concept of *Standortgebundenheit*.

8. See hereto Morgenthau's early lectures on Aristotle in the 1947 winter term at the University of Chicago (especially that of February 20) where he understands realism, rationalism, and empiricism (also idealism) as epistemologies, while realism means for him primarily the social, political, and historical contextualization of theory and agency rather than the analysis of, and action in, reality due to abstract principles.

9. With reference to his *Scientific Man vs Power Politics* (1946) he notes that "(it) must suffice here [i.e., 1962a] to state dogmatically that the object of social sciences is man, not as a product of nature but as both the creature and creator of history in and through which his individuality and freedom of choice manifest themselves" (p. 27). And in his Second of his "Six Principles ... " he argues: "Political realism ... requires ... a sharp distinction between the desirable and the possible – between what is desirable everywhere and at all time and what is possible under the concrete circumstances of time and place."

10. Most explicit here may be Schütz and his differentiation between two levels of social "reality" and respective constructions (see Schütz, *Collected Papers I*, "The Problem of Social Reality"; also his *The Phenomenology of the Social World*, which appeared originally in German as *Der sinnhafte Aufbau der sozialen Welt* in 1932).

11. See here most explicitly his article "The Limitations of Science and the Problem of Social Planning" (1944).

12. Similar to Max Weber's critique of "ethics of conviction" ("*Gesinnungsethik*") opposing an "ethics of responsibility"; however,

Morgenthau does not refer to Weber, as his references to Weber in general are very rare. Arguing here against universal moral standards does *not* mean that Morgenthau would be principally against them; indeed, his normative preferences for world order are committed to the idea of universal standards. However, under the conditions and contexts of politics in the 20th century and the particularistic fragmentation of the world into nation-states, he simply does not deem universal standards possible and he sees the attempt to institutionalize these as creating more problems (i.e., war and violence) than solutions (see in this regard also his PhD from 1929, his *Habilitation* from 1934(a) and 1962b, 1962c).

13. This critique found its continuation in Morgenthau's dismissal of the Vietnam War; among many pieces of evidence, see a letter from Morgenthau to Kissinger, dated October 22, 1968. In this context of Morgenthau's attempts to correct his perception by Kissinger and others, from the later 1950s onwards, he also pointed frequently to his *Dilemmas of Politics*, Chapter 4 (1958a), where he had revisited and clarified his position. For the above reasons, he also declined many requests to reprint "The Primacy of National Interest" in textbooks, readers, and editions.

14. See Morgenthau, 1945a, p. 145: "For it is utopian to assume that a rational system of thought by its own inner force can transform the conditions of man, it is no less utopian to expect that a stable, peaceful society can be built on power." And in an unpublished manuscript titled "How Immoral is Political Realism" (1952b), we read: "We can make moral progress only by working with the forces that shape the world, not against them."

15. See hereto Morgenthau's lectures on Aristotle (2004), held from 1970–73 at the New School; also his unpublished Aristotle lectures at the University of Chicago, already as of winter 1947.

16. This may not just have been due to un-reflected usage of certain terms, but due to the encounter with and sometimes unreconciled clash between two very different intellectual worlds and socializations in Morgenthau – a continental-European and an American Anglo-Saxon – in which the same terminologies have sometimes very different meanings and are by no means immediately translatable; more on this below regarding Morgenthau's use of "objectivity" and "power".

17. He explicitly argues against the Hobbesian picture of "*homo homini lupus*"; see Morgenthau, 1945b, and an unpublished manuscript in German on "*Über die Herkunft des Politischen aus der Natur des Menschen*" (i.e., "*The Derivation of the Political from Human Nature*"; translation by Morgenthau himself noted on the manuscript in handwriting).

18. As well as religion and love/sociability; however, he puts much more emphasis, at least in his later writings, on power than on love and religion.

19. In manuscripts written in German, such as "*Der Selbstmord mit gutem Gewissen*" (i.e., "Suicide with a Good Conscience") or "*Über die Herkunft des Politischen aus der Natur des Menschen*", Morgenthau speaks of "Kraft" and "Tatkraft" when referring to humankind's longings towards religion, love, and power; this is why the terminology of "power" seems to us to

be another example of a distortion resulting from translation (for which, of course, Morgenthau is responsible himself) and why "puissance" and "potency" seem much better suited. See more on this below in Chapter 4 under "Morgenthau's Twofold Concept of Power".

20. Because of the importance of the concept of power for Morgenthau's political theory, we have added a whole chapter on his concept of power; see below Chapter 4 of this Introduction under the heading "Morgenthau's Twofold Concept of Power".

21. See the entry "Max Weber", *Stanford Encyclopedia of Philosophy*, 2007; also Ringer (1997) on Weber's epistemology.

22. Interesting here is Morgenthau's discussion of objectivity in an unpublished manuscript – written in German – on *Metaphysik* and ethics, where he distinguishes between three types of objectivity: scientific, normative, and empirical. All three forms are to be understood as categories of knowledge (*"Eigenschaft der Erkenntnis"*). Thus, objectivity depends upon which concepts are used to recognize and analyze the qualities of an object, which are, however, inherent in and emerging from the object and which are made visible (only) *in relation* to the concepts applied.

23. As also argued elsewhere; see Behr (2005); Behr/Heath (2009).

4　Morgenthau's Twofold Concept of Power

1. Historicism is to be distinguished from historism. We follow here Stefan Berger's definition: "I deliberately use the term 'historism'...rather than 'historicism'...Whereas 'historism' (...*Historismus*)...can be seen as an evolutionary, reformist concept which understands all political order as historically developed and grown, 'historicism' (*Historizismus*), as defined and rejected by Karl Popper, is based on the notion that history develops according to predetermined laws towards a particular end" (2001, p. 28; emphasis in the original).

2. The *Hermannsdenkmal* was started in 1841 and finished in 1875. It commemorates the victory of the Cherusci over the Romans in 9AD. The *Kyffhäuser* Monument was built between 1890 and 1896 on top of the Kyffhäuser mountain in Thuringia. According to a legend, the medieval king, Friedrich I "Barbarossa" is said to reside in this mountain. The *Völkerschlachtsdenkmal*, finally, was finished in 1913 and commemorates the battle of the nations in 1813, in which Prussian, Austrian, Russian, and Swedish troops had beaten the French troops of Napoleon Bonaparte.

References

Adorno, Theodor W. and Horkheimer, Max (1981 [1944/1947]), *Dialektik der Aufklärung*, ed. Rolf Tiedemann, Frankfurt: Suhrkamp.

Adorno, Theodor W. and Horkheimer, Max (1992), "Odysseus or Myth and Enligtenment", *New German Critique*, No. 56, Special Issue on Theodor W. Adorno, pp. 109–41.

Alexander, Samuel (1960), "The Basis of Realism", in R. Chisholm (ed.) *Realism and the Background of Phenomenology*, Illinois: Free Press of Glencoe, pp. 186–222.

Amstrup, Niels (1978), "The 'Early' Morgenthau: A Comment on the Intellectual Origins of Realism", *Cooperation and Conflict*, Vol. 13, No. 2, pp. 163–75.

Arendt, Hannah (1953), "Ideology and Terror: A Novel Form of Government", *Review of Politics*, Vol.15, No. 3, pp. 303–27.

Arendt, Hannah (1958), *The Human Condition*, Chicago: University of Chicago Press.

Arendt, Hannah (1969), "Reflections on Violence", reprinted from the *New York Review of Books*, 27 February.

Arendt, Hannah (1970), *On Violence*, Orlando: Harcourt.

Arendt, Hannah (1978), "We Refugees", in Ron H. Feldman (ed.), *Hannah Arendt: The Jew as Pariah. Jewish Identity and Politics in the Modern Age*, New York: Grove Press, pp. 55–66.

Arendt, Hannah and McCarthy, Mary (1995), *Im Vertrauen. Briefwechsel 1949–1975*, ed. Carol Brightman, Munich: Piper.

Aristotle (2009), *Nicomachean Ethics*, trans. David Ross, rev. with an introduction and notes by Lesley Brown, Oxford: Oxford University Press.

Ashley, Richard and Walker, R. B. J. (1990), "Introduction: Speaking the Language of Exile: Dissident Thought in International Studies", *International Studies Quarterly* 34 (3), Special Issue: Speaking the Language of Exile: Dissidence in International Studies, pp. 259–68.

Bain, William (2000), "Deconfusing Morgenthau: Moral Inquiry and Classical Realism Reconsidered", *Review of International Studies*, No. 26, pp. 445–64.

Barboza, Amalia (2006), "Distanzierung als Beruf: Karl Mannheims soziologischer Ansatz als 'Innovationstendenz' der deutschen Soziologie", in Amalia Barboza and Christoph Henning (eds), *Deutsch-Jüdische Wissenschaftsschicksale. Studien über Identitätskonstruktionen in der Sozialwissenschaft*, Bielefeld: Transcript, pp. 232–55.

Barkawi, Tarak (1998), "Strategy as a Vocation: Weber, Morgenthau and Modern Strategic Studies", *Review of International Studies*, No. 24, pp. 159–84.

Behr, Hartmut (2005), "Misreading in International Relations Theory. Ideologiekritische Anmerkungen zum Realismus und Neo-Realismus", *Zeitschrift für Politikwissenschaft*, Vol. 15, No. 1, pp. 61–90.

Behr, Hartmut (2010) *A History of International Political Theory: Ontologies of the International*, Basingstoke/New York: Palgrave Macmillan.

Behr, Hartmut and Heath, Amelia (2009), "Misreading in IR Theory and Ideology Critique: Morgenthau, Waltz, and Neo-realism", *Review of International Studies*, Vol. 35, No. 2, pp. 327–49.

Behr, Hartmut and Rösch, Felix (2010), "Comparing 'Systems' and 'Cultures': Between Universalities, Imperialism, Indigenousity", in Hans Joachim Lauth (ed.), *Vergleichende Regierungslehre: Eine Einführung – Comparative Politics: An Introduction* (3rd edn), Opladen: VS-Verlag, pp. 73–91.

Benjamin, Walter (1999), *Illuminations: Edited and with an Introduction by Hannah Arendt*, London: Pimlico.

Berger, Stefan (2001), "Stefan Berger responds to Ulrich Muhlack", *German Historical Institute London Bulletin*, Vol. 23, No. 1, pp. 21–33.

Cozette, Muriel (2008), "Reclaiming the Critical Dimension of Realism: Hans J. Morgenthau and the Ethics of Scholarship", *Review of International Studies*, Vol. 34, No. 1, pp. 5–27.

DeRose, Keith (2009) *The Case for Contextualism*, Oxford: Oxford University Press.

'Descartes' Epistemology' (2005) *Stanford Encyclopedia of Philosophy*, Stanford, CA: Stanford University Press.

Descartes, René (1996) *Discours de la methode; and Mediations on first philosophy*, ed. David Weissman, New Haven: Yale University Press.

Eckstein, George (1981), "Hans Morgenthau: A Personal Memoir", *Social Research*, Vol. 48, No. 4, pp. 641–52.

Edkins, Jenny (1999), *Poststructuralism and International Relations: Bringing the Political Back In*, Boulder, CO: Lynne Rienner.

Eisfeld, Rainer (1991), *Ausgebürgert und doch angebräunt: Deutsche Politikwissenschaft 1920–1945*, Baden-Baden: Nomos.

Falk, Richard A. (1984), "Normative Constraints on Statecraft: Some Comments on Morgenthau's Perspective", in Kenneth W. Thompson (ed.), *Truth and Tragedy: A Tribute to Hans J. Morgenthau*, Piscataway, NJ: Transaction, pp. 77–84.

Feldmann, Richard (1999) "Contextualism and Skepticism", *Nous*, Supplement: *Philosophical Perspectives*, "Epistemology", No. 13, pp. 91–114.

Feldmann, Richard (2001) "Skeptical Problems, Contextualist Solutions", *Philosophical Studies*, Vol. 103, No. 61, pp. 61–85.

Forndran, Erhard (1997), "Grenzen des Realismus. Zu Erklärungsversuchen internationaler Beziehungen. Teil II: Zur Reichweite realistischer Argumentation", *Zeitschrift für Politikwissenschaft*, Vol. 7, No. 1, pp. 33–77.

Frankfurter, Felix (1937), "Letter to Nathan Greene", December 9 (unpublished manuscript, Manuscript Division, Library of Congress, Washington, DC, Box 22).

Frei, Christoph (1994), *Hans J. Morgenthau: Eine intellektuelle Biographie*, Bern: Paul Haupt.

Frei, Christoph (2001), *Hans J. Morgenthau: An Intellectual Biography*, Baton Rouge: Louisiana State University Press.

Frei, Christoph (2005), "Hans J. Morgenthau's Early Quest", in Christian Hacke et al. (eds), *The Heritage, Challenge and Future of Realism: In Memoriam Hans J. Morgenthau (1904–1980)*, Göttingen: V & R, pp. 39–48.

Freud, Sigmund (1953), *Civilisation, War and Death*, London: Hogarth Press.

Freud, Sigmund (1961), *The Standard Edition of the Complete Psychological Works of Sigmund Freud. Volume XXI. The Future of an Illusion. Civilization and its Discontents and Other Works*, London: Hogarth Press.

Fromkin, David (1993), "Remembering Hans Morgenthau", *World Policy Journal*, Vol. 10, No. 3, pp. 81–8.

George, Jim (1994), *Discourses of Global Politics: A Critical (Re)Introduction to International Relations*, Boulder, CO: Lynne Rienner.

Giddens, Anthony (1984), *The Constitution of Society*, Cambridge: Polity Press.

Good, Robert C. (1960), "The National Interest and Political Realism: Niebuhr's 'Debate'with Morgenthau and Kennan", *Journal of Politics*, Vol. 22, No. 4, pp. 597–619.

Guzzini, Stefano (1998), *Realism in International Relations and International Political Economy: The Continuing Story of a Death Foretold*, London: Routledge.

Hacke, Christian (2005), "Power and Morality: On the Legacy of Hans J. Morgenthau", *American Foreign Policy Interests*, Vol. 27, No. 3, pp. 171–4.

Hall, Ian (2006), "World Government and Empire: The International Historian as Theorist", *International Affairs*, Vol. 82, No. 6, pp. 1155–65.

Hayward, N. F. and Morris, D. S. (1988), *The First Nazi Town*, Aldershot: Avebury.

Hirst, Paul (2001), *War and Power in the 21st Century: The State, Military Conflict and the International System*, Oxford: Polity Press.

Hobsbawm, Eric (1990), *Nations and Nationalism since 1780: Program, Myth, Reality*, Cambridge: Cambridge University Press.

Hoeber-Rudolph, Susanne (2005), "The Imperialism of Categories: Situating Knowledge in a Globalizing World", *Perspectives on Politics*, No. 3, pp. 5–14.

Hoffmann, Stanley (1977), "An American Social Science: International Relations", *Daedalus*, No. 106, pp. 41–60.

Holt, E. B. et al. (1960), "Introduction to the New Realism", in R. Chisholm (ed.), *Realism and the Background of Phenomenology*, Illinois: Free Press of Glencoe, pp. 151–85.

Jütersonke, Oliver (2010), *Morgenthau, Law and Realism*, Cambridge: Cambridge University Press.

Kindermann, Gottfried-Karl (2004), "In Memorian Hans J. Morgenthau", *Internationale Politik*, No. 2, pp. 85–6.

Kissinger, Henry (1980), "Hans Morgenthau: A Gentle Analyst of Power", *New Republic*, No. 83, pp. 12–14.

Kleinschmidt, Harald (2004), *Carl Schmitt als Theoretiker der internationalen Beziehungen*, Hamburg: Helmut Schmidt Universität.

Koskenniemi, Martti (2000), "Carl Schmitt, Hans Morgenthau, and the Image of Law in International Relations", in Michael Byers (ed.), *The Role of Law in International Politics: Essays in International Relations and International Law*, Oxford: Oxford University Press, pp. 17–35.

Koskenniemi, Martti (2004), *The Gentle Civilizer of Nations: International Law 1870–1960*, Cambridge: Cambridge University Press.

Lebow, Richard Ned (2003), *The Tragic Vision of Politics: Ethics, Interests, and Orders*, Cambridge: Cambridge University Press.

Lévinas, Emmanuel (1996), "Meaning and Sense", in Adrian T. Peperzak, Simon Critchly, Robert Bernasconi (eds), *Basic Philosophical Writings*, Bloomington and Indianapolis: Indiana University Press, pp. 35–64.

Loader, Colin (1997), "Free Floating: The Intelligentsia in the Work of Alfred Weber and Karl Mannheim", *German Studies Review*, Vol. 20, No. 2, pp. 217–34.

Lukács, György (1963), *The Theory of the Novel: A Historic-philosophical Essay on the Forms of Great Epic Literature*, London: Merlin Press.

Mannheim, K. (1936), *Ideology and Utopia*, London: Routledge.

Mannheim, K. (1984), "Die Methoden der Wissenssoziologie", in Kurt Lenk (ed.) *Ideologiekritik und Wissenssoziologie*, Frankfurt: Campus, pp. 203–12.

Marcuse, Herbert (1964), *The One-Dimensional Man: Studies in the Ideology of Advanced Industrial Society*, Herbert Marcuse Archive (cartoon.iguw.tuwien.ac.at/christian/marcuse/odm.html; July, 10, 2011).

Métall, Rudolf Aladár (1969), *Hans Kelsen. Leben und Werk*, Vienna: Franz Deuticke.

Mollov, M. Benjamin (1997), "Jewry's Prophetic Challenge to Soviet and other Totalitarian Regimes according to Hans J. Morgenthau", *Journal of Church and State*, No. 39, pp. 561–75.

Molloy, Seán (2004), "Truth, Power, Theory: Hans Morgenthau's Formulation of Realism", *Diplomacy and Statecraft*, Vol. 15, No. 1, pp. 1–34.

Morgenthau, Hans J. (1929), *Die internationale Rechtspflege, ihr Wesen und ihre Grenzen*, Leipzig: Robert Noske.

Morgenthau, Hans J. (1930a), "Stresemann als Schöpfer der deutschen Völkerrechtspolitik", *Die Justiz*, Vol. 5, No. 3, pp. 169–76.

Morgenthau, Hans J. (1930b), "Der Selbstmord mit gutem Gewissen. Zur Kritik des Pazifismus und der neuen deutschen Kriegsphilosophie" (unpublished manuscript, Manuscript Division, Library of Congress, Washington, DC, Box 96).

Morgenthau, Hans J. (1930c), "Über die Herkunft des Politischen aus dem Wesen des Menschen" (unpublished manuscript, Manuscript Division, Library of Congress, Washington DC, Box 151).

Morgenthau, Hans J. (1932), "Der Kampf der deutschen Staatslehre um die Wirklichkeit des Staates" (unpublished manuscript, Manuscript Division, Library of Congress, Washington DC, Box 110).

Morgenthau, Hans (1933), *La notion du "politique" et la théorie des différends internationaux*, Paris: Recueil Sirey.

Morgenthau, Hans J. (1934–35), "Einige logische Bemerkungen zu Carl Schmitts Begriff des Politischen" (unpublished manuscript, Manuscript Division, Library of Congress, Washington DC, Box 151).

Morgenthau, Hans J. (1934a), *La réalité des normes : En particulier des normes du droit international. Fondement d'une théorie des normes*, Paris: Félix Alcan.

Morgenthau, Hans J. (1934b), "Über den Sinn der Wissenschaft in dieser Zeit und über die Bestimmung des Menschen" (unpublished manuscript, Manuscript Division, Library of Congress, Washington DC, Box 151).

Morgenthau, Hans J. (1936), "Positivisme mal compris et théorie réaliste du droit international", in Silvio A. Zavala (ed.), *Colección de estudios históricos, jurídicos, pedagógicos y literarios. Homenaje a D. Rafael Altamira*, Madrid: C. Bermejo, pp. 1–20.

Morgenthau, Hans J. (1937), "Kann in unserer Zeit eine objektive Moralordnung aufgestellt werden? Wenn ja, worauf kann sie gegründet werden? Kennwort: Metaphysik" (unpublished manuscript, Manuscript Division, Library of Congress, Washington DC, Box 112).

Morgenthau, Hans J. (1944), "The Limitations of Science and the Problem of Social Planning", *Ethics*, Vol. 54, No. 3, pp. 174–85.

Morgenthau, Hans J. (1945a), "The Machiavellian Utopia", *Ethics*, Vol. 55, No. 2, pp. 145–7.

Morgenthau, Hans J. (1945b), "The Evil of Politics and the Ethics of Evil", *Ethics*, Vol. 56, No. 1, pp. 1–18.

Morgenthau, Hans J. (1946 [also 1974]), *Scientific Man vs Power Politics*, Chicago: University of Chicago Press.

Morgenthau, Hans J. (1947a), "Letter to Rita Neumeyer Herbert", June 2 (Manuscript Division, Library of Congress, Washington DC, Box 26).

Morgenthau, Hans J. (1947b), Lectures on Aristotle, Winter term 1947, University of Chicago. *Hans J. Morgenthau Archive*, Library of Congress, Washington DC, Box 76.

Morgenthau, Hans J. (1948), "Letter to Michael Oakeshott", May 22 (Manuscript Division, Library of Congress, Washington DC, Box 44).

Morgenthau Hans J. (1949a), Lecture on "Philosophy of International Relations", also held 1952, University of Chicago (*Hans J. Morgenthau Archive*, Library of Congress, Washington DC, Box 81).

Morgenthau, Hans J. (1949b), "National Interest and Moral Principles in Foreign Policy: The Primacy of the National Interest", *American Scholar*, No. 18.

Morgenthau, Hans J. (1950–59), Letters in Relation to his article "The Primacy of National Interest" during the 1950s (*Hans J. Morgenthau Archive*, Library of Congress, Washington DC, Box 97).

Morgenthau, Hans J. (1952a), "Building a European Federation. The Schuman Plan and European Federation", *Proceedings of the American Society of International Law*, No. 46, pp. 130–4.

Morgenthau, Hans J. (1952b), "How Immoral is Political Realism" (unpublished manuscript *Hans J. Morgenthau Archive*, Library of Congress, Washington DC, Box 98).

Morgenthau, Hans J. (1954), "The Yardstick of National Interest", *Annals of the American Academy of Political and Social Science*, No. 296, pp. 77–84.

Morgenthau, Hans J. (1955), "Reflections on the State of Political Science", *Review of Politics*, Vol. 17, No. 4, pp. 431–60.

Morgenthau, Hans J. (1958a), *Dilemmas of Politics*, Chicago: University of Chicago Press.

Morgenthau, Hans J. (1958b), "Letter to Edward Dew", August 22 (Manuscript Division, Library of Congress, Washington DC, Box 17).

Morgenthau, Hans J. (1959a) "The Nature and Limits of a Theory of International Relations",in W. Fox (ed.), *Theoretical Aspects of International Relations*, Notre Dame: Notre Dame University Press, pp. 15–28.

Morgenthau, Hans J. (1959b), "Education and World Politics", *Daedalus*, No. 88, pp. 121–38.

Morgenthau, Hans J. (1959c), "Dilemmas of Politics", *International Affairs*, Vol. 35, No. 4, p. 502.

Morgenthau, Hans J. (1960a), "The Social Crisis in America: Hedonism of Status Quo", *Chicago Review*, Vol. 14, No. 2, pp. 69–88.

Morgenthau, Hans (1960b), "The Problem of German Reunification", *Annals of the American Academy of Political and Social Science*, No. 330, pp. 124–32.

Morgenthau, Hans J. (1961), Letter to Gottfried-Karl Kindermann, April 5 (*Hans J. Morgenthau Archive*, Library of Congress, Washington DC, Box 33).

Morgenthau, Hans J. (1962a), "The State of Political Science", in Hans J. Morgenthau (ed.) *Politics in the Twentieth Century, Vol. I, The Decline of Democratic Politics*, Chicago: University of Chicago Press, pp. 16–35.

Morgenthau, Hans J. (1962b), "The Intellectual and Political Functions of a Theory of International Relations", in Hans J. Morgenthau (ed.) *Politics in the Twentieth Century, Vol. I, The Decline of Democratic Politics*, Chicago: University of Chicago Press, pp. 62–78.

Morgenthau, Hans J. (1962c), "The Commitments of a Theory of International Politics", in Hans J. Morgenthau (ed.) *Politics in the Twentieth Century, Vol. I, The Decline of Democratic Politics*, Chicago: University of Chicago Press, pp. 55–61.

Morgenthau, Hans J. (1962d), *Politics in the Twentieth Century, Vol. I, The Decline of Democratic Politics*, Chicago: University of Chicago Press.

Morgenthau, Hans J. (1962e), "Love and Power", *Commentary*, March, published by the American Jewish Committee, pp. 247–51.

Morgenthau, Hans J. (1962f), "Letter to Richard S. Cohen", October 4 (Manuscript Division, Library of Congress, Washington DC, Box 10).

Morgenthau, Hans J. (1962g), *Politics in the Twentieth Century, Vol. III, The Restoration of American Politics*, Chicago: University of Chicago Press.

Morgenthau, Hans J. (1963), *Macht und Frieden: Grundlegung einer Theorie der internationalen Politik*, Gütersloh: C. Bertelsmann Verlag.

Morgenthau, Hans J. (1965), *Vietnam and the United States*, Washington DC: Public Affairs Press.

Morgenthau, Hans J. (1968a), Letter to Henry Kissinger, October 22 . *Hans J. Morgenthau Archive*, Library of Congress, Washington DC, Box 76.

Morgenthau, Hans J. (1968b), "Letter to Bryon Dobell", July 9 (Manuscript Division, Library of Congress, Washington DC, Box 43).

Morgenthau, Hans J. (1970), *Truth and Power: Essays of a Decade, 1960–1970*, London: Pall Mall Press.

Morgenthau, Hans J. (1971), "Power as a Political Concept", in R. Young (ed.), *Approaches to the Study of Politics*, Evanston: Northwestern University Press, pp. 66–77.

Morgenthau, Hans J. (1972), *Science: Servant or Master?*, New York: New American Library.

Morgenthau, Hans J. (1973), "Macht und Ohnmacht des Menschen im technologischen Zeitalter", in Oskar Schatz (ed.), *Was wird aus dem Menschen? Der Fortschritt – Analysen und Warnungen bedeutender Denker*, Graz: Verlag Styria, pp. 47–60.

Morgenthau, Hans J. (1976), "Hannah Arendt 1906–1975", *Political Theory*, Vol. 4, No. 1, pp. 5–8.

Morgenthau, Hans J. (1978), "Six Principles of Political Realism", *Politics Among Nations: The Struggle for Power and Peace* (also 1954, 1960, 1963, 1985), New York: Knopf.

Morgenthau, Hans J. (1979), *Human Rights and Foreign Policy*, New York: Council on Religion and International Affairs.

Morgenthau, Hans J. (1984), "Fragment of an Intellectual Autobiography: 1904–1932", in Kenneth W. Thompson (ed.), *Truth and Tragedy: A Tribute to Hans J. Morgenthau*, Piscataway, NJ: Transaction, pp. 1–17.

Morgenthau, Hans J. (1985), *Politics among Nations. The struggle for power and peace*, New York: Alfred A. Knopf.

Morgenthau, Hans J. (2004), *Political Theory and International Affairs: Hans J. Morgenthau on Aristotle's The Politics*, Westport, CT: Praeger.

Morgenthau, Hans J. (1984), "Postscript to the Transaction edition: Bernard Johnson's interview with Hans J. Morgenthau", in Kenneth W. Thompson (ed.), *Truth and Tragedy: A Tribute to Hans J. Morgenthau*, Piscataway, NJ: Transaction, pp. 333–86.

Morgenthau, Hans J. and Warburg, James P. (1960), "The Problem of German Reunification", *Annals of the American Academy of Political and Social Science*, No. 330, pp. 124–32.

Münkler, Herfried (2009), *Die Deutschen und ihre Mythen*, Berlin: Rowohlt.

Murray, A. J. H. (1996), "The Moral Politics of Hans Morgenthau", *Review of Politics*, Vol. 59, No. 1, pp. 81–107.

Neacsu, Mihaela (2010), *Hans J. Morgenthau's Theory of International Relations: Disenchantment and Re-enchantment*, Basingstoke: Palgrave Macmillan.

Nietzsche, Friedrich (1968), *The Will to Power*, New York: Vintage.

Nietzsche, Friedrich (1969), *Thus spoke Zarathustra: A Book for Everyone and No One*, London: Penguin.

Nietzsche, Friedrich (1990), *On the Advantages and Disadvantages of History for Life*, Hackett: Indianapolis.

Nietzsche, Friedrich (2003), *The Gay Science: With a Prelude in German Rhymes and an Appendix of Songs*, Cambridge: Cambridge University Press.

Nobel, Jaap W. (1995), "Morgenthau's Struggle with Power: The Theory of Power Politics and the Cold War", *Review of International Studies*, Vol. 21, No. 1, pp. 61–85.

Osterhammel, Jürgen (2009), *Die Verwandlung der Welt: Eine Geschichte des 19. Jahrhunderts*, Munich: C. H. Beck.

Pichler, Hans-Karl (1998), "The Godfathers of 'Truth': Max Weber and Carl Schmitt in Morgenthau's Theory of Power Politics", *Review of International Studies*, No. 24, pp. 185–200.

"Rationalism vs Empiricism" (2008), *Stanford Encyclopedia of Philosophy*, Stanford, CA: Stanford University Press.

Ringer, Fritz (1969), *The Decline of the German Mandarins: The German Academic Community, 1890–1933*, Cambridge, MA: Harvard University Press.

Ringer, Fritz (1997), *Max Weber's Methodology: The Reunification of Cultural and Social Sciences*, Cambridge, MA: Harvard University Press.

Ringmar, Erik (1996), *Identity, Interest and Action: A Cultural Explanation of Sweden's Intervention in the Thirty Years War*, Cambridge: Cambridge University Press.

Ringmar, Erik (2006), "Liberal Barbarism and the Oriental Sublime: The European Destruction of the Emperor's Summer Palace", *Millenium: Journal of International Studies*, Vol. 34, No. 3, pp. 917–33.

Rohde, Christoph (2004), *Hans J.Morgenthau und der weltpolitische Realismus*, Wiesbaden: VS Verlag für Sozialwissenschaften.

Rosa, Hartmut (2009), "Social Acceleration: Ethical and Political Consequences of a Desynchronized High-speed Society", in Hartmut Rosa and William E. Scheuerman (eds), *High-speed Society: Social Acceleration, Power, and Modernity*, University Park: Pennsylvania State University Press, pp. 77–111.

Rösch, Felix J. (2011), "Hans J. Morgenthau, the Marginal Man in International Relations: A 'Weltanschauungsanalyse'", PhD thesis, submitted April, Newcastle University, School of Geography, Politics and Sociology.

Scheuerman, William E. (1999), *Carl Schmitt: The End of Law*, Lanham: Rowman & Littlefield.

Scheuerman, William E. (2007), "Was Morgenthau a Realist? Revisiting Scientific Man vs Power Politics", *Constellations*, Vol. 14, No. 4, pp. 506–30.

Scheuerman, William E. (2009), *Hans Morgenthau: Realism and Beyond*, Cambridge: Polity Press.

Schmitt, Carl (1996), *The Concept of the Political*, Chicago: University of Chicago Press.

Schuett, Robert (2007), "Freudian Roots of Political Realism: The Importance of Sigmund Freud to Hans J. Morgenthau's Theory of International Power Politics", *History of the Human Sciences*, Vol. 20, No. 4, pp. 53–78.

Schütz, Alfred (1944), "The Stranger: An Essay in Social Psychology', *American Journal of Sociology*, Vol. 49, No. 6, pp. 499–507.

Schütz, Alfred (1962) *Collected Papers I*, 'The Problem of Social Reality', The Hague: MartinusNijhoff.

Schütz, Alfred (1967) *The Phenomenology of the Social World*, London: Heinemann Educational (1932 as *Der sinnhafte Aufbau der sozialen Welt*).

See, Jennifer W. (2001), "A Prophet Without Honour: Hans Morgenthau and the War in Vietnam, 1955–-1965", *Pacific Historical Review*, Vol. 70, No. 3, pp. 419–47.

Shilliam, Robbie (2007), "Morgenthau in Context: German Backwardness, German Intellectuals and the Rise and Fall of a Liberal Project", *European Journal of International Relations*, Vol. 13, No. 3, pp. 299–327.

Simmel, Georg (1964), "The Stranger", in Kurt H. Wolff (ed.), *The Sociology of Georg Simmel*, New York: Free Press, pp. 402–8.

Simmel, Georg (1995), *Philosophie der Mode. Die Religion. Kant und Goethe. Schopenhauer und Nietzsche. Gesamtausgabe Band 10*, Frankfurt: Suhrkamp.

Sinzheimer, Hugo (1932), "Letter to Hans J. Morgenthau", March 11 (Manuscript Division, Library of Congress, Washington DC, Box 197).

Snyder, Jack (2011), "Tensions with Realism: 1945 and After", in Nicolas Guilhot (ed.), *The Invention of International Relations Theory: Realism, the Rockefeller Foundation and the 1954 Conference on Theory*, New York: Columbia University Press, pp. 54–78.

Spinks, Lee (2003), *Friedrich Nietzsche*, London: Routledge.

Tjalve, Vibeke Schou (2008), *Realist Strategies of Republican Peace: Niebuhr, Morgenthau, and the Politics of Patriotic Dissent*, Basingstoke: Palgrave Macmillan.

Tucker, Robert W. (1952), "Professor Morgenthau's Theory of Political 'Realism'", *American Political Science Review*, Vol. 46, No. 1, pp. 214–24.

Turner, Stephen P. (2009), "Hans J. Morgenthau and the Legacy of Max Weber", in Duncan Bell (ed.), *Political Thought and International Relations: Variations on a Realist Theme*, Oxford: Oxford University Press, pp. 63–82.

Turner, Stephen and Mazur, George (2009), "Morgenthau as Weberian Methodologist", *European Journal of International Relations*, Vol. 15, No. 3, pp. 477–504.

Vierhaus, Rudolf (1972), "Bildung", in Otto Brunner, Werner Conze and Reinhart Koselleck (eds), *Geschichtliche Grundbegriffe: Historisches Lexikon zur politisch-sozialen Sprache in Deutschland. Band 1*, Stuttgart: Klett-Cotta, pp. 508–51.

Vollrath, Ernst (1987), *Grundlegung einer philosophischen Theorie des Politischen*, Würzburg: Königshausen und Neumann.

Wasserman, Benno (1959), "The Scientific Pretensions of Professor Morgenthau's Theory of Power Politics", *Australian Journal of International Affairs*, Vol. 13, No. 1, pp. 55–70.

Weber, Max (1978), *Economy and Society: An Outline of Interpretative Sociology. Volume I*, Berkeley: University of California Press.

Weber, Max (2004), *The Vocation Lectures: Science as a Vocation. Politics as a Vocation*, Indianapolis: Hackett.

Williams, Michael C. (2004), "Why Ideas Matter in International Relations: Hans Morgenthau, Classical Realism, and the Moral Construction of Power Politics", *International Organization*, Vol. 58, No. 4, pp. 633–65.

Williams, Michael C. (2005), *The Realist Tradition and the Limits of International Relations*, Cambridge: Cambridge University Press.

Young-Bruehl, Elisabeth (1982), *Hannah Arendt: For Love of the World*, New Haven: Yale University Press.

Part II

The Concept of the Political and the Theory of International Disputes

Hans J. Morgenthau

Translator's Note

Maeva Vidal

The translation of Morgenthau's *La notion du "politique" et la théorie des différends internationaux* was a challenge, not only because of the complexity and depth of Morgenthau's writing, which we have endeavored to carefully preserve, but also because of the challenges posed by the language of the original text. Indeed, Morgenthau's writing in *La notion du "politique"* is often complicated and sometimes ambiguous. This is due largely to the writing style, which uses long, labyrinthine sentences with multiple clauses and sub-clauses, but also to certain editorial oversights in the original text (e.g., missing or erroneous punctuation, missing pronouns). As with any translation, the task at hand consisted not only in rendering the original French text into its English equivalent, but most importantly in interpreting Morgenthau's words for an English-speaking reader. This is an important nuance, as in order to properly convey the meaning of the text it was sometimes necessary to diverge slightly from the original French. For example, some sub-clauses were placed in the notes rather than in the body of the text; some redundancies found in the French were edited to tighten the language. One important departure is the merger of the third chapter of the original French (titled "De la notion de différend d'intérêt"), which was less than a page long, into the last section of Chapter 2 of the English text. Another includes the addition of a subtitle ("Excursus: 'tension', 'dispute' and the concept of the political") in Chapter 4 to delineate what is clearly a subsection of the main argument. These and other minor deviations improve the readability and the clarity of *The Concept of the Political*, and scholars should rest assured that the translator and the editors have endeavored to ensure that the meaning of the English text is faithful to the original. To further clarify the text, important terms, such as Morgenthau's differentiation of power into force (*pouvoir*) and puissance (*puissance*), but also many more, are presented to the reader both in our English translation and in the original French in brackets and italics. Endnotes which were inserted by the translator and/or the editors are clearly indicated as such to differentiate them from Morgenthau's notes; these additional notes include more specific comments on individual sentences, terms, references, and quotations. Note also that the footnote style from Morgenthau's original French text has been converted into Harvard style. Finally, the language chosen for the translation was American English, as this was the language in which Morgenthau himself communicated and published after his emigration to the United States.

Preface

Certain elements of the theory elaborated herein were already touched upon in *International Judicature, its Nature and Limits*.[1] They are presented here in a more complete and in-depth manner, particularly with regard to their sociological foundation, and also with certain modifications and additions. We have limited ourselves to the most essential bibliographical indications, and refer to the detailed notes of the above-cited work for the remainder.

The following developments are of an exclusively theoretical nature. They relate only to the classification of international disputes and to the sociological structure which forms their basis. No practical conclusions of any sort are drawn from these empirical findings, especially concerning the justiciability of international disputes. We find it necessary to emphasize this last point, as the dominant doctrine tends to confuse empirical and normative points by identifying juridical disputes with justiciable disputes, as well as political disputes with non-justiciable disputes, being then tempted to draw certain immediately practical conclusions solely from classification. Such conceptualization would lead to a misinterpretation of the spirit of the present work; I refer on this point to the indications given in the last chapter, which I propose to further develop at a later date.

1
Introduction

The question which we propose to discuss is of unusual timeliness in today's field of international jurisdiction as it touches on the distinction between legal and political disputes. The settlement of disputes is, moreover, one of the fundamental problems that any fully developed (*complet*[1]) legal system is tasked to resolve, along with the delimitation of respective powers (*pouvoirs*) and their spheres of activity, as well as with the regulation of transformation of power and the guarantee of its execution.

In the state's domestic sphere, the legal system must be able to answer the four following questions: who holds legal power over any given object, say, for example, a desk? In what manner can the holder of the legal power be changed? How can a dispute, the object of which concerns the legal power, be resolved? Finally, in what manner will the holder of the legal power be protected in the course of exercising this power? A legal system which, in the domestic sphere, could not give an answer to the first of these questions would also no longer have any objective basis with which to find the solution to the other three questions. Moreover, in the absence of an answer to the second question, the legal system would come into conflict with the living forces which call for modifications in the spheres of powers, and this conflict could prove fatal to the said legal system. In addition, if the legal system does not provide an answer to the third question, its constitutive elements will not progress beyond the state of theoretical principles and will never be able to materialize themselves in practice, in such a way that, in the absence of this preliminary condition, it will no longer be possible to ensure the legal system's sanction. Finally, if the legal system omits to answer the fourth and last of these questions, its objective decisions, as well as the system itself, would run the risk of remaining ineffectual. Only by answering these four questions can a legal system be capable of accomplishing the task which falls to any legal system, which is to ensure justice and peace.[2]

However, it is only to the first of these questions that international law, in its own sphere, provides a more or less clear and adequate answer. The answers it provides to questions two and four are absolutely inadequate, and consequently the answer to question three remains largely devoid of practical effectiveness, despite being satisfactory in theory. Such are the problems, mentioned here in passing, with regard to which the classification of international disputes takes on particular significance. For it is in the identification of the concept of legal litigation with that of justiciable litigation, on the one hand, as well as the identification of the concept of the political with that of matters which could not be brought to legal bodies, on the other hand, that the above-mentioned inadequacy of international law in the justiciable becomes apparent. However, the scope of the problem of distinguishing legal and justiciable (e.g., political) litigation exceeds the sphere of international jurisdiction because the concept of the political touches the very legal and sociological foundations of international law. Moreover, this problem is found in the domestic sphere of the state where it presents itself as a problem of jurisdiction in domestic political disputes, and again we find that here the concept of the political takes on major importance in the system of domestic public law.

In any case, we do not propose to broach here all of these fundamental problems, as they are the subject of a book in preparation.[3] We will limit ourselves for now to outlining the problem of the classification of international disputes, while trying in particular to draw out a tentative definition of the concept of the political which is the basis of all these fundamental problems.

2
On the Concept of Legal Disputes

The definition of the concept of legal disputes does not present any great theoretical interest in present legal scholarship.[1] At most, this definition is important because in practice, the obligation to submit international disputes to legal settlement or arbitration is most often limited to those international disputes which are also legal disputes, a limit placed without any theoretical grounding.[2] This means that the doctrine, in which some confusion appears to prevail regarding the possibilities and conditions of a classification of international disputes, has lent considerable undeserved attention to legal disputes by devoting numerous and meticulous studies to their practice.

Furthermore, there are differences in this doctrine regarding the criterion which would permit a clear delimitation of the sphere of legal disputes. We have agreed to recognize that the concept of the legal matter cannot be taken in the strict sense of an opposition to the concept of the question of fact. For both the theory of international jurisdiction and its practice as well as procedural law in general, show that questions of fact (such as the amount of compensation for which the principle was admitted upon merit) are precisely those issues that enter unquestionably into the realm of competence of any legal body adjudicating in strict law. We have also agreed to recognize that the qualifier "legal dispute" must apply only to disputes that bear a certain relation to the norms of international law. However, opinions differ as soon as there is the question of specifying the nature of this relation.

Two schools of thought have manifested themselves on this issue: for some, there must be a direct relation between the dispute and a norm of international law, with this relation becoming henceforth an objective relation. From this point of view, "legal disputes are disputes susceptible to being resolved according to the principles of the law".[3] For others, however, the criterion must be sought in the relation between the dispute and the norm of international law such that it results from the parties' own declarations. Leo Strisower says thus:[4] "Legal disputes should be considered those in which both parties believe that according to the law, their claim constitutes a legal claim, in other words that it is based on existing law, or that it constitutes a preliminary question for a claim of this nature... The difference in this case (compared to conflicts of interest or political conflicts) results from (in accordance with the Hague Conventions) the fact that the concept of conflict is no longer understood here as being determined by the objective content of the reciprocal claims, but by the manner in which these claims are presented and motivated." Johan Castberg is also of the opinion that the criterion of the concept of legal disputes lies "in the manner in which the parties themselves have presented the issues which form the object of the dispute."[5]

The difference between these two formulations may well influence the solution to the problem. However, it is far from being as important as commonly held. The definition of legal disputes as disputes susceptible of a decision according to the principles of law contains an unknown. It does indeed state that the relation between the dispute and the legal norm consists in the norm being applicable to the dispute; it remains silent, however, concerning the question of knowing on which basis it will be possible to decide, in each particular case, whether or not the dispute is susceptible to being decided by virtue of a legal norm. The object of the dispute itself, in other words the content of the claim put forward, does not permit a conclusion to be drawn. For example, should State A require from State B the cession of City C, invoking the principle of national self-determination, this will not constitute a legal dispute for the principle of national self-determination is not a rule of general positive law. However, if State A grounds its claim on a treaty concluded with State B, insisting on its enforcement, and if the existence of this treaty were not contested by State B the dispute becomes a matter susceptible of a decision by virtue of the rules of the law of nations, in the present case according to the principle of "pacta sunt servanda" as well as by virtue of the arrangements of the said treaty, applicable according to the general principles of the law of nations on the interpretation of treaties.

The advantage of the formulation which relates to the declarations of the parties over the one which has just been considered thus consists in the more precise designation of the grounds used to determine the relation between the legal norm and the dispute. In other words, the first formulation is more complete than the second, which, though theoretically admissible, remains nonetheless imprecise and incomplete since it omits to take into account, in the connection between the norm and the dispute, the intermediary link consisting of the declarations of the parties.

The two formulations have the following in common: besides the subjective element occasioned by the declarations of the parties, both formulations bring into play an objective criterion – that of the concept of the legal dispute. For it is ultimately the possibility of resolving the dispute on the basis of the norms of positive international law which constitutes, for both formulations, the criterion of the concept of the legal dispute. Each of these two methods of discrimination stems, as from a factual certainty, from the concept of the norm of international law. However, there precisely lies the fundamental problem, a problem which could not, we believe, be the object of a universally accepted solution in the present state of international law and legal scholarship.

Any consideration of the concept of the legal dispute necessarily leads to the question of the concept of law in general, and we can consequently see all the difficulties that are raised by defining the content of the concept of law, especially in international law. It will suffice, for the purposes of this study, to mention the group of problems known as "pure positivism – sociological method – natural law", as well as the problem of codification, and establish that a precise determination of the concept of legal disputes is subordinate to a clear and universally valid definition of the concept of international law and the limits of its sphere.[6]

Having explained the theoretical foundations that should guide us in expressing the concept of the legal dispute, it is now possible to broach a consideration of the concept itself. The criterion of the concept of legal disputes lies in the possibility of ruling on the dispute by virtue of the rules of international law; this possibility results in turn from the manner in which the parties formulate their claims. It would thus be possible to say that legal disputes consist of all the disputes which, on the basis of the declarations of the parties, can be decided by virtue of the principles of the law. The obvious weak point of such a definition is that it places the criterion of the possibility of resolving a dispute according to the rule of law not in the objective nature of the dispute itself, but in the subjective declarations of the parties. If we accept this definition, the parties then become free to bestow a legal nature on their dispute solely through their own will, thus making it into a legal or a non-legal dispute as they please. Any state wishing to assert a claim legally without merit and based solely on considerations alien to the law could in this way, through political maneuvering, transform the dispute into a legal proceeding, thus extracting an objective decision from an international legal body simply because it pleased the state to ground its claim on legal considerations, for example on a treaty.[7]

It is very clear that a definition which could in practice lead to such a result is inadequate. For, in making the qualification of a given dispute dependent solely on the parties' own will – in such a way that a given litigation could equally be, according to the whim of the parties, a legal dispute or a simple divergence of interests – the definition in fact would eliminate a demarcation which it had been called upon to draw, countering the goal which it must serve, namely to allow both parties of an agreement to know from the beginning the exact scope of the obligations they are assuming.[8]

In order to fulfill its practical goal, a definition of the concept of legal disputes must establish an objective criterion allowing one to distinguish, from amongst the allegations of the parties invoking legal motives, between those allegations that obviously cannot rely on positive law and those for which the relation with positive law cannot be allowed without scrutiny. The following two circumstances, that the sole will of the parties is not sufficient to bring or not to bring a dispute into the sphere of legal disputes and that in addition an objective criterion is a necessity, are already brought to light by the fact that in many adjudication treaties, the question of knowing whether a dispute enters into one or the other of these two categories is left to the assessment of an international legal body. As a legal decision can only intervene on the basis of the application of an adequate general rule to a specific case, for the said clause to make sense and to have some practical scope, there must in all necessity exist a general rule, in other words an objective one on the basis of which an international legal body can make its decision concerning the group in which the dispute must be categorized. When it is commonly said that this objective criterion of the nature of a dispute resides in the concept of international law, we presumably get closer to solving the problem. However, we have already seen that, with such a general observation, we can hardly pursue the consideration of the question to its furthest and most decisive elements. For if the norms of international law allow one to say whether, yes or no, the allegations of one party invoke existing rules of law, they are not, however, sufficient to pronounce on the very nature of this legal motivation, because they do not provide any direct reference point with which to discriminate between various claims in this category.

Such a criterion is found in the definitions of B. Mulder and J. H. W. Verzijl. According to the former, there exists a legal dispute "every time there is *reasonable* belief that a legal matter divides the parties."[9] The latter defines legal disputes as those "where the parties on both sides rely on arguments which cast doubts, *prima facie reasonable*, on the issue of knowing whether objective international law recognizes, or not, the existence of the subjective rights invoked by one party and contested by the other or others."[10] For both, the criterion for the distinction between real or alleged legal disputes thus lies in whether or not a dispute would appear, according to reasonable views, legal at first sight. It is certain that the principles of reason are objective norms, but they are obviously the most general norms known to science. This characteristic of generality is precisely why these principles preside as fundamental principles over scientific research in general, but it is also why, however, they do not lend themselves well to being essential elements of a specific definition.[11] For, ultimately, any claim which is not sufficiently grounded in law appears to be unreasonable, and the criterion of the distinction between legal and non-legal disputes would then reside only in the degree to which the nature of a legally ill-founded claim is unreasonable. Thus seems to be, moreover, the opinion of Verzijl when he speaks about "doubts prima facie reasonable."

In order to better clarify the nature of the doubt which must exist concerning the admissibility of a claim from the point of view of positive law, and for this doubt to be qualified as "reasonable" (in other words to define the conditions required for the qualification of a dispute as a legal dispute to appear reasonable at first sight), let us refer to an example which has already been useful to us several times. State A requires from State B the cession of City C, invoking a treaty which provides in some obscure clause for a change in sovereignty concerning City C. It would be completely reasonable here to consider that doubts persist on the point of knowing whether the claim is grounded, and it would thus be reasonable to consider that here is a legal matter which divides the parties. It would again be the same in a case where the claim relied on a treaty which is not historically contested, but of which the application to the case in question could be contested on considerations of time or space.

The situation would be completely different, however, in a case where State A required from State B the cession of City C while grounding itself on a treaty despite the fact that no treaty providing for a transfer of sovereignty of City C exists or has ever existed, neither in law, nor in fact. The characteristic element in the latter case is that it would not even be possible to uphold a legal controversy on the preliminary question of the existence or the non-existence of the treaty invoked. The claim does indeed base itself on legal arguments, as it invokes a treaty, but the assertion that such a treaty exists and that it would constitute a norm of international law could not be upheld legally. For the possibility of defending the validity of a norm of law by using legal arguments presupposes at least that the general legal principles of the validity of international law can, in one way or another, apply to the alleged facts. In other words, in our case, this would mean that there exists objectively at the very least a document with the alleged content, even if it is only a written sheet of paper. It would thus not be possible, in our case, to uphold a legal controversy on the preliminary question of the existence or the non-existence of a norm of law taking on the form of a treaty. Any attempt by a body of jurisdiction to consider the case from a legal point of view, under any aspect whatsoever, would be here objectively impossible. It does appear at first sight contrary to the principles of reason to speak in this case of a *legal* dispute, or to have the least doubt concerning the attitude of international law regarding a claim of this nature.

Thus doubt, with regards to the recognition of a given case by positive international law, will only be reasonable in the case where the dispute concerns the interpretation or the application of a legal rule of which the existence cannot be denied; or when the denial concerns the preliminary question of the existence of a legal rule and when the arguments of the parties are based on considerations taken from law. Hence we can say that even when the parties base themselves on legal arguments, there will nevertheless not be a legal dispute if the arguments in question are based on legal rules of which the existence could not be legally upheld. *Legal disputes are thus disputes which reveal, with regard to the considerations motivating the assertions of the parties, a divergence of opinion on a point susceptible to a decision by virtue of a legal rule which is incontrovertible, or of which the existence can at the very least be upheld using legal arguments.*[12]

Because international law does not allow in the current state of its development the delimitation of the sphere of legal disputes within a clear and precise definition, it has been endeavored to remedy the situation by substituting the method of enumeration to that of the general clause. This means that it is not the general concept of the legal dispute which is the object of the contractual obligation, but rather a catalogue of the principal types of legal disputes. Thus has been proposed a whole series of formulations which at times differ quite significantly in their content. Two of these formulations have passed into practice. They are:

1. The formulation of the Franco-English Treaty of Arbitration dated October 14, 1903: "Disputes of a legal nature *or* relating to the interpretation of existing treaties between the two contracting Parties..." This definition is scientifically untenable, for it is clear that disputes relating to the interpretation of treaties do not go beyond the sphere of legal disputes of which they even constitute an important part.
2. The formulation of Article 13, Paragraph 2 of the *Covenant of the League of Nations*, reproduced in Article 36 of the Statute of the Permanent Court of International Justice, as well as in a number of arbitration treaties: "Disputes related to (a) the interpretation of a treaty, (b) any point of international law, (c) the reality of any fact which, if it were established, would constitute the severance of an international commitment, (d) the extent or the nature of the reparation due for such a severance."

The second formulation also calls for serious criticism from a theoretical point of view. The group included under the letter (b) "any point of international law", the sphere of which could not be broader, encompasses the three other groups as well. It is thus not acceptable to place this formulation on the same level as the other groups. In addition, an enumeration which limits itself to a boundless number of cases, some of which are quite special, such as those in groups (c) and (d), necessarily remains quite incomplete and could not have an "exemplificative" nature. This is what Jean Ray states: "In order to achieve it completely (Art. 13), it would be necessary to conceive an almost complete progression (*cours*) in international law."[13] And even leaving aside the theoretical critiques called for by this formulation, its practical scope would still be of the most limited kind. For the difficulties to which the definition of the concept of legal disputes is up against will be present here, in a more limited framework but still retaining the same scope, when it is time to define each of the various enumerated groups. We must also add the following dilemma which any enumeration necessarily entails: the more general the enumeration, the less it will fulfill the characteristic of precision which the enumeration entails; inversely, the more it enters into details, the more it will be difficult to make it complete. The only real usefulness of such an enumeration is to illustrate the concept of the legal dispute, and this goal will be better attained through the insertion into treaties of a clause of a *general* nature, accompanied by a list of cases given only as examples.

It is common practice in the dominant doctrine to oppose the concept of disputes of *interest* to that of legal disputes, defining in this way the whole of the disputes which are not susceptible to a decision on the basis of a legal norm. We do not propose, in this terminological analysis, to examine the practical value of this distinction which is minimal, as has been shown elsewhere.[14] We will thus limit ourselves to establishing that, from a terminological point of view, such an opposition is not correct, as legal disputes are also disputes of interest, in other words disputes having as an object an interest (i.e., a *political* interest) which pits one party against another. These disputes are legal because they possess the characteristics of the concept of the legal dispute as we have established, while the so-called disputes of interest do not.[15] It would thus be more correct to name the latter 'pure disputes of interest.'

3
The Concept of the Political

On the subjective concept of the political

The object of the concept of the political is diverse. In the original and etymological sense, this concept enters into the sphere of public life, but everyday language sometimes applies it in relation to non-state actors, or even to individuals. We are concerned here with the definition of the concept of the political in the sphere of interstate relations. Our considerations are solely concerned with the sphere of foreign policy. Applied to state relations, the concept of the political designates something which concerns the "polis", the state taken as such, in accordance with the concept's etymological sense and with its most widespread usage. In the sphere of international relations, political matters are thus those which are likely to have an influence on the relation of one state with other states – that is, on the situation of one state within the international community.[1]

However, any external action by the state ultimately concerns its relations with other states, and considering their goals, all external actions are always political.[2] We therefore cannot base the criterion for the difference between political matters and non-political matters solely on the relation to the state, especially when we are looking to define a concept which not only encompasses a distinct part of international relations, but all the more when looking for the meaning of a general concept of the political.

Some have alleged that the difference between political matters and non-political international matters resides in the fact that the first did not possess a legal nature, and therefore that the criterion should lie in the particular form of the political action by which the state pursues the fulfillment of its political ends. The concept of the political would thus be equivalent to that of matters of pure interest. However, following empirical examination, it appears that such a differentiation is not founded because the historical record abounds with cases in which legal matters have taken on an unmistakably political nature. Thus, the question of knowing whether the territorial integrity of China was violated by Japan in 1931 is of great political importance despite its legal nature. The same is true of the Franco-German dispute of 1911 regarding Morocco; of the issue of the legitimacy of the occupation of a vast part of the Chinese province of Shantung by Japanese troops in 1928; of the issue of the legitimacy of the allied intervention in Greece during the world war;[3] of the Rumanian-Hungarian dispute in the matter of optants *etcetera*.

It would not be more correct to say, inversely, that a dispute of which the object is not governed by international law, and which is thus a dispute of pure interest, must necessarily possess a political nature due to this absence of legal rule. For example, fixed rules concerning the extent of the "domaine réservé"[4] do not exist in international law; however, disputes regarding this matter would, despite this, not generally be considered *political* disputes. The historical record thus proves that the opposition of legal and political matters, accepted in the doctrine, does not exist in reality. The assertion of the legal nature of a dispute does not necessarily imply that it does not have a political nature. *The concepts of the political and of the legal definitely do not constitute an antithetic pair. The opposite concept to that of the political matter can be found in the concept of the non-political matter, and not in that of the legal matter. In turn, the latter can be both of a political nature as well as of a non-political nature.*[5]

If we relinquish the idea of considering the relation to positive international law as a distinguishing feature between political and non-political matters, there is still another criterion left to establish this distinction, a criterion which resides in the very object of the matters fitting into one or the other of these groups. Those scholars in favor of this last conceptualization take it for granted that, owing to the nature of their object, certain matters never take on a political characteristic, whereas other matters, for the same reason, always present such a characteristic. They consider, however, that the former are always of a legal nature. These colleagues do, however, set themselves apart from the opinion examined above by the fact that it is not the legal nature of a dispute which leads them to decide on its non-political nature, but rather that they base themselves on an objective criterion.

The proposals made by Russia at the First Peace Conference in The Hague (1899) stem from this conceptualization, as well as those made by Switzerland and a host of other countries at the Second Peace Conference in The Hague (1907), with the aim of developing a list enumerating nonpolitical matters. But such a list lost all significance, even from the point of view of the conceptualization considered here, as soon as a clause was added concerning matters of honor or vital interests, as called for by the Russian draft. For either the matters enumerated in this list do not possess any political characteristic by virtue of their nature, which would make the clause superfluous, or these matters are, just like those which do not appear on the list, political matters (or those that can at the very least *become* political). Thus, if the addition of the so-called honor and vital interest clause is justified, it becomes, however, completely useless to draw up a list of matters which, on this point, do not distinguish themselves in the least from the others. Nevertheless, insofar as these proposals anticipated the establishment of a list of matters which must be submitted to arbitration, without conditions or restrictions, the unconditional recognition of the principle of arbitration for disputes relating to these matters implied the observation that these disputes could never be of a political nature. For, according to the states represented at The Hague Conferences, disputes of a political nature could not have been the object of an obligation to arbitration. The matters proposed for this list involved the most varied domains. At the Second Peace Conference in The Hague it was finally decided by majority that the list would be comprised of the following matters.

First, disputes bearing on the interpretation or the application of conventions concerning free reciprocal relief provided to indigent patients; international protection of workers; measures to prevent collisions on the open sea; weights and measures; measurements of ships; wages and belongings of deceased sailors; protection of works of art and literary works. And, *second*, claims for damages in cases where the parties are in agreement on the principle of compensation.

All of these matters resemble each other in that from the point of view of the position of the state within the international community, their importance is more or less secondary and the interests that they bring into play are limited to specific cases. It is an empirical fact that disputes of this kind lead much more rarely to serious international complications than, for example, matters of minority, economic problems, and territorial questions; in other words, all matters which are usually qualified as political. But is it appropriate to conclude from this indisputable difference concerning their political nature that there is cause to distinguish between the concepts of these two groups of disputes, in that the ones should be considered always and everywhere as being of a political nature, and that the others should be without any exception considered non-political disputes? In other words, would these two categories of disputes correspond to different concepts?

Experience proves the contrary. For example, the paper of the Peruvian delegation at the Second Pan-American Conference of 1902 states that: "Within America, border matters do not lead, in reality, to political disputes. They are matters of a purely technical nature...In America, there do not exist, strictly speaking, treaties of a political nature. It would be quite difficult to quote one."[6] Matters which we Europeans are accustomed to qualifying as political are thus not, as a general rule, considered as such in South America. What's more, that is a conceptualization which would probably be difficult to maintain today. The political nature of these matters thus depends on circumstances of time and place and does not result from a ground of principle. On the other hand, it would be entirely possible to admit in theory that on the day when the problem of minorities finds an adequate solution, matters of minority would lose their political nature; that it would be the same for economic matters should the problem of economic relations ever be appropriately settled; and that generally, all matters considered political today would lose this characteristic should the circumstances which bestow this political nature upon them ever come to be modified. Thus, there exists no matter that can be once and for all qualified as "political" which would possess this characteristic by its very nature. All that can be said, based on experience, is that in specific circumstances, which are as yet unknown, certain issues regularly acquire a political characteristic, which they would in no way possess under other circumstances.

The same observation must be made, but the other way around, concerning matters which have been definitely classified as nonpolitical matters at the Second Peace Conference at The Hague, and which were proposed for the aforementioned list. Non-political character in no way results from the very nature of these matters. It is only a fact of experience: experience regular enough to take on the appearance of a fixed rule, but of which the fairly numerous exceptions nevertheless attest to its exclusively empirical origin which does not derive from the concept of the political itself. Thus, for example, in the Casablanca affair the object of the dispute would not have in itself justified the qualifier "political". Nonetheless, following special circumstances, the dispute did take on a distinctly political nature. The same can be said for the Rumanian-Hungarian dispute regarding optants. It is a fact of experience that the matters which formed the object of these two litigations do not always possess a political nature, and that, in any case, they do not regularly possess this characteristic. Thus, the political nature they assumed in both of the historical cases in question did not derive from the natures of the disputes themselves – it is rather explained by other reasoning.

The debates at the Second Peace Conference at The Hague concerning which matters should feature on the list, and the rather meager results which were achieved, prove moreover that there is no agreement within the consciousness of states on what constitutes the sphere of matters which can be definitely classified as nonpolitical. Certain matters which one state, from the point of view of its particular interests, considered as lacking all political character, seemed to some other state, based on its particular interest, to possess a political character, or at least to be susceptible to possessing one.[7] The list that was finally established was a rather reduced one compared to what was initially proposed, and it would besides have had only minimal practical significance. It was moreover adopted only by majority vote with the result that it did not even pass into effective international law.[8]

We must thus conclude that it is impossible to establish a distinction between political and nonpolitical matters according to their object, since the concept of the political is not necessarily inherent to certain specific objects, just as it is not necessarily absent from other specific objects. The sphere of political disputes thus cannot be defined once and for all by referring to the nature of the matters it encompasses; no matter can be considered necessarily political owing to its object, but any matter can *acquire* a political nature following circumstances external to its object. The concept of the political does not have a fixed content which can be determined once and for all. It is rather a *quality*, a tone, which can be peculiar to any object and which attaches itself with some preference to certain objects, but which does not by necessity attach itself to any of them. Certain matters take on this tone with a particular ease and frequency, but no matter possesses this tone on its own, by sole virtue of its nature.[9] A given matter, considered to be political today, could no longer possess this characteristic tomorrow, while some other matter could suddenly become a prime political issue. Besides the more or less restricted sphere of matters with a relatively permanent political nature which can be considered *first class political issues* (such as border, minority or economic issues), there exists a vast sphere of matters which clearly reveal this floating political nature, a nature which manifests itself intermittently here and there without ever attaching itself definitely anywhere.[10] This is the sphere of *second class political issues*.

We could ask ourselves: in what consists this particular quality or tone possessed by matters which we consider to be political? Provided that this quality does not cleave to its object, what possibility has been left to define it?

We began with the observation that political matters are those which bear a connection to the state. We had also established that such a definition, based on the etymological meaning, went too far and besides did not correspond to the common usage. A more precise concept of the political, fitting into the general concept, should possess the elements of the concept of the political in the broad and etymological sense of the word, but should also distinguish itself from this sense through particular characteristics, highlighting the specific qualities of the strict sense of the concept of the political. We must thus determine, within as it were the general concept of the political, a concept where political nature would be expressed with more clarity and more strength. If we have thus been able to observe from the political in general that its specific element lies in the fact that the object of the state's activity is connected to the state, it follows that, if we keep to what we have just stated concerning the relation between a general and a specific definition, *the criterion of the difference between the two kinds of connections which can exist between the object of an action of the state and the state, and which correspond to*

the two concepts of the "political", one general (etymological) and one spe-
cific (complying with the literal meaning of the word), lies in the degree of
intensity of the connections between the object of the state's activity and
the state.[11, 12] Where this connection is closer (more direct), there will
be political matters in the strict sense (in the literal sense).

The characteristic element of this concept of the political thus
resides solely in a tone, in a particular nuance, in the absence of any
substantial character. The political is a quality which can be found,
to varying degrees, in all subject matter, just like the quality of heat
can be found in all bodies; and just like we cannot say that it is of
a body's essence to be hot unlike other bodies, we can no more say
about a given subject matter of international relations that it possesses, by its very nature, a political character. In one case like in
another, it is only a question of intensity, the degree of which varies
with the circumstances that determine this intensity. There is only
one difference: with the aid of a mercury column and a graduated
scale, we can objectively measure the degree of the heat of a body at
a moment in time. But in the political sphere, there is no such objective measure. We can certainly, in each particular case, evaluate the
degree of intensity with which one object or the other of the activity
of the state touches the state, basing our judgment on a rather reliable feeling which rests on the continual experience which we have
concerning the various degrees of intensity. However, it is impossible
to delineate the concept of the political with a precision such that
it would be possible to state the following in advance: when such
and such rationally determinable elements are given, we will be in
the presence of a political matter. Whatever effort we make to find
a rational definition of the political, which would permit the determination of the political nature of a dispute – simply by verifying,
on the sole basis of a logical examination, whether certain elements determined in advance are fulfilled in a given concrete case (in
other words, by means of a logical subordination) – there will always
remain a remnant (represented by the particular degree of intensity)
which could *not* be the object of an objective measure.[13] This remnant would seem to escape any scientific definition, and could only
be assessed by way of feeling.[14]

And yet, if the political nature (in the literal sense) of an interstate
dispute consists in the particularly high degree of intensity of the
connection of the state to the object of the dispute and if, moreover,

the political element is but a simple quality of the subject matter, a quality which is in no way inherent to its essence, we must consequently ask ourselves: due to which logically determinable facts can this same subject matter, at a given moment in history, be particularly closely connected to the state, while at another moment in history, this same connection can once again loosen itself completely from the state? How can we then explain that certain international disputes should always be of a political nature, while others only rarely present this characteristic? What is the principle (*loi*[15]) that governs the increase of intensity of this connection to the state, and what governs its decrease?

On the objective concept of the political

The efforts made until now to logically define the various types of international disputes have failed,[16] and this counts even for those that had the most value from a scientific point of view, such as those by Hersch Lauterpacht[17] and by Dietrich Schindler.[18] All of these attempts were necessarily destined to fail, it seems, for they aimed to outline a demarcation between legal and political disputes, without preoccupying themselves first with defining, even only approximately, the content of the concept of the political. The dominant theory, prisoner of the positivist prejudice according to which legal problems can only be resolved through the interpretation of positive law (any scientific research going beyond this being no longer in the sphere of legal science), has attempted to solve the problem simply by defining the concept of the political as the opposite of the concept of the legal matter or the matter susceptible of a legal solution. According to this theory, the concept of the legal matter, or of the matter susceptible to a legal settlement, already implies the concept of the political, which is only its opposite. For as we have seen, this theory considers that any matter which is not legal, in other words which is not susceptible to a legal settlement, is thus by definition a political matter. An author like Schindler himself, who possesses, as we shall later see, an accurate feeling as to what makes the essence of our problem, defines the concept of the political by basing himself on the classic construct of the separation of powers, by the opposition of the legislative and the executive to the judiciary: "The executive and legislative functions ... , in other words the political functions."[19]

The classic expression of the dominant theory, with the obvious proof of its sterility regarding the solution to our problem, will nonetheless be found in a "theory" – if we can name it thus – which would not deserve to be considered in itself but which imposes itself on our attention owing to the quality of its authors and of the corresponding quality of the argumentation. This argument is in itself perfect, wonderfully characterizes the dominant doctrine, and claims to bring a solution to the problem[20] (a claim which, by the fact of its authors' authority, must be taken seriously). This "theory" consists in the proposal made in 1922 by the Institute of International Law.[21] The part of the proposal which interests us here states: "Art. 2. However, when according to the opinion of the state summoned in a legal matter the dispute is not susceptible to be settled by legal processes, the preliminary question as to whether the dispute is justiciable is submitted for review to the Permanent Court of International Justice which will rule on the question according to its usual procedure."

The Institute contents itself with proposing to leave it to the Permanent Court of International Justice, which will have to decide whether an issue is or is not susceptible to legal settlement. The report by Marshall-Brown and Politis, which was used as the basis for the Institute's proposal, explicitly dismisses any statement of the problem which would take into account the concept of the political in its literal sense. But, as remarked by Hans Wehberg, we can, from any political dispute, extract what he very correctly calls "the legal merit." Consequently, the problem of the classification of matters of a justiciable nature comes back to determining if they are appropriate to being brought before a Court of Law. What matters in this regard is not the political interest which may be at stake; it is the "legal merit" of the dispute. In other words, while the statesman may not be disposed to submit certain matters to legal consideration, the legal scholar must only ask himself whether the matter is "susceptible" to a legal decision by application of the principles of law.[22]

By qualifying as political that aspect of the problem which, according to us, is the only essential one, and by making it solely the object of discussions between statesmen, this report goes well beyond what we wanted to say here about the imprecise nature of the concept of the political, a nature which is rebellious to any technical-legal definition. The report refuses to the problem any possibility of it being the object of exact scientific research, under any connection whatsoever, from the point of view of international law. For this report, this problem is already in the sphere of the arbitrary, "of apprehensions, of ideas, of feelings",[23] where the legal scholar must avoid to venture. The Institute even refuses to broach the subject of the problem of the specific nature of political matters and chooses to deal solely with those concepts which can be based on international positive law, a choice which is incidentally in accordance with a tendency also represented in the doctrine of domestic public law. The Institute – of which the resolution implies the idea that the imperfection of international law does not manifest itself in those spheres which are precisely amongst its most important and which, in theory, correspond to the concept of the political in international relations – has not only left the problem of the demarcation of legal and political matters unsolved, contrary to what it thought it had achieved, it has in addition failed to even make progress on the solution.

The Institute – supported by its indisputable authority – has rather directed this fundamental problem of international "*jus pacis*" to the side-track of procedure, and has contented itself with a banal and inconsistent proposal which is not even an attempt at a solution and to which Max Huber's exhortation made five years later to the Institute – that in any case, purely platonic resolutions should be avoided – would apply very well. By acting in this manner the Institute has obscured the problem, much more than it has shed light on it.[24]

The repugnance with which the dominant theory regards all matters which are not susceptible to being resolved on the basis of a legal text obviously renders quite difficult the solution to the problem of the classification of international disputes. For it is impossible to establish a demarcation between two concepts, when in fact we only know the content of one of the concepts, and also when this positivist method only allows us to determine one of them. This method knows, so to speak, only one dimension, reaching only the superficial layer of the legal formations which overlie social relations. The social element which underlies the legal system inevitably escapes this method, and this method is thus inevitably inapplicable to the problems which have as their object precisely those connections which exist between this underlying social element and the legal system superimposed upon it.

The concept of the political is in fact precisely one of those concepts with regard to which positivist dogma is found lacking; for this concept is not of a legal nature, and rather falls under the sphere of social reality. It is certainly susceptible to being the object of a legal ruling, which is even indispensable for maintaining peace. Nevertheless, it does not belong as such to the sphere of legal concepts. We do not propose to intervene in the discussion which the publications of Benedetto Croce,[25] Richard Kroner (1931), Helmuth Plessner (1931), Rudolf Smend (1928), and Carl Schmitt (1932) have opened on the philosophical and sociological foundations of the concept of the political. We will limit ourselves here only to the indispensable psychological and sociological remarks.

The notion of the political, taken in the broadest sense of the word, applies itself to manifestations which go widely beyond the sphere of the state. We can thus speak about the politics of a city, about those of a cartel, an association, and even about the politics of an individual, such as, for example, the politics of a man practicing a profession toward his colleagues or his clients, or those of a debtor toward his creditors, or those of a woman toward her husband, the world or her servants. All of these sociological established facts have this in common: they all have the will to power as the psychological factor at their base. When we assign the term 'political' to the activity which these persons expend as part of the social relations in question, we mean by this that this activity is the expression of their will to power. It is true that in common parlance it is always implied that the subject of this will implements great mental resources to reach their goal; if they do not apply some thought to it, or if they resort to physical force, we will no longer say in everyday language that they are "doing politics."

This will to power can take on three different aspects: it can aim to maintain acquired power, to increase it, or to manifest it. The individual which does politics in the general sense seeks either to: preserve the sphere of influence which they already possess; expand their influence beyond this sphere, regularly invoking, to justify this tendency, their superior qualities and the corresponding needs; or simply establish, in their own eyes and in the eyes of those other members of the social group to which they belong, the entire expanse of their sphere of influence in order to thus assert the success of their will to power and to renew the satisfaction felt when this will is realized. This search for satisfaction predominates in all human activity. However, in the present case in which there is a will to assert one's power, it presents a rather particular aspect from the point of view of its connection to its object. While the will to maintain and the will to increase one's power relate one and the other to objects which in themselves have an objective value independent of the will in question, the will to assert one's power, however, shows in its object an often grotesque disproportion between the object's objective value and the intensity of the will which relates to it. This particular characteristic of the will to assert one's power, which distinguishes it from the two other aspects of the will to power, has found classic expression in the words of Hamlet: "Rightly to be great / Is not to stir without great argument, / But greatly to find quarrel in a straw / When honour's at the stake."

However, contrary to the conceptualization of the sociological and psychological elements of the political which we have sketched out here, a concept which we soon hope to be able to outline more fully, the following has been asserted:

> We can reach a definition of the concept of the political only after having first established and then determined what are the specific categories that fall under this concept. Political nature has indeed its own criteria. These manifest themselves and remain distinct from those belonging to the other spheres which are relatively independent of human action and thought, for example, in particular, Morality, Aesthetics, or Economy. It is thus appropriate to search for the criteria of the political in certain final elements of differentiation which are particular to it and to which could be connected any political action in the specific sense. We can accept, for example, that in the sphere of morality, everything leads back to the distinction between good and evil; that aesthetics rest on the opposition of the beautiful and the ugly; and that economy rests on the opposition of the useful and the harmful, or if we prefer, on that of good and bad yields. The question then becomes to know whether there also exists, in the sphere of the political, a principle of differentiation which, without necessarily being of the same nature and of the same scope as those above, would nevertheless like them possess an independent and autonomous nature, and could then serve as a simple and immediately

apparent criterion of political nature. What could this criterion be? The specifically political opposition to which all political acts and motives relate in the end is that of the enemy and the friend. This results in a definition of the concept from the point of view of its criterion, but not in a complete definition which exhausts its content. And, to the extent that this distinction does not itself rest on some other criterion, it would provide, in the sphere of the political, an equivalent to the more or less independent criteria of good and evil in the system of morality, of beautiful and ugly in the system of aesthetics, etc.[26]

If we believe that we should proceed here with an in-depth exam of the logical merits of Carl Schmitt's concept, it is not only because of the considerable agency it has exerted on public opinion, but also because it has served as a basis for a metaphysics of the role played by elementary forces in international relations; metaphysics which, according to Schmitt, would result with inescapable necessity from his concept of the political driven to its most final consequences. It is quite obvious that such a construct of the political should, if it were grounded, exert the greatest influence on the theory of international disputes.

We could not presume to "refute" a metaphysical construct by proving that its assertions do not agree with the known empirical facts. For in a case where they do not at all stray from sensory reality, they no longer retain anything metaphysical. We would only have cause to invoke such a contradiction if we were attempting to establish that such and such a supposedly scientific doctrine does not possess this characteristic, but is rather in reality metaphysical. However, as we have stated numerous times, Schmitt's doctrine is a metaphysical one which only very distantly appeals to historical and psychological reality.[27] And towards a doctrine whose metaphysical nature is no longer in question, we can adopt only two attitudes: either we match against it different metaphysics and thus critique it in the name of a transcendental principle, which amounts to abandoning scientific grounds ourselves in favor of metaphysical ones; or, we seek to draw out some logical contradiction in the principles or the deductions of the doctrine in question, while showing that the goal proposed by the author of such a doctrine could never be reached by the means which he has implemented or that the conclusions of his theory are in contradiction with its premise. In this latter case, the critique will be immanent, based on the theory itself and not on some adverse and uncontrollable principle. This critique will have a scientific nature because it rests on the general principles of logic.

However, we recognize neither the theoretical necessity for a definition of the concept of the political to have recourse to the system of categories conceived by Schmitt, nor the logical correctness of those he has proposed for the sphere of the political. From the point of view of the specific concept and nature of morality, for example, or of aesthetics, the oppositions of good and evil, beautiful and ugly etc., do not express anything more than what already resulted from the words which designate these concepts. The concepts of morality and aesthetics, just like those of the political and the economic, serve indeed to establish two different types of distinctions. On the one hand, they mark the boundary, of one in relation to the other, of the various spheres of the political, the economic, the moral or the aesthetic; the fundamental oppositions reside here in the concept pairs of moral–nonmoral (in other words, moral on one side and aesthetic, political etc. on the other), political–nonpolitical (political–economic, aesthetic etc.), and so forth for the other spheres.

But besides this distinction of the different spheres in relation to each other, there also exists a second distinction, logically different from the first, which concerns the discriminations we can establish within each of these spheres, on the basis of the measure of the values which is particular to each of them. Schmitt concerns himself solely with this latter problem when, in the sphere of the political, he seeks out the fundamental distinction which would correspond to those of good and evil, beautiful and ugly etc. in the other spheres. It is, however, from the point of view of the first of the two distinctions which we have established, in other words from the distinction of these various spheres in relation to each other, that Schmitt takes into account the antithetic pairings of good and evil, beautiful and ugly etc.; for these various distinctions which are established *within* each particular sphere are at the same time, in the eyes of Schmitt, the characteristic signs which permit one to distinguish each sphere *one from the other*. It is thus solely from the point of view of this problem that the various distinctions in question acquire any importance in his eyes; it remains nonetheless true that in fact it is solely these distinctions which constitute for him the object of his research. And it is in the solution of this last problem that he believes he can find, at the same time, the solution to the other problem.

However, the determination of this group of distinctions does not in fact constitute a real problem, as the measures of value in question result directly from the concepts themselves. The measure of the values which serves to determine the distinctions within the sphere of the aesthetic could only by necessity be this concept of the aesthetic itself, for it is precisely the distinction established from the point of view of this aesthetic measure which permits the delimitation of the sphere of the aesthetic from the other spheres. This, however, does not mean that its content is in any way determined and characterized in relation to that of the other spheres. In other words, according to whether a given object complies or not with the measures of value implied by the concept of the aesthetic, it will be judged as having, or not having, an aesthetic value, or to wit, as being aesthetic or nonaesthetic, or, finally, as beautiful or ugly.

The same can be said in the sphere of morality, where the final distinctions can equally only be established on the basis of the concept itself; what complies with the measures of value implied by the concept of morality will be considered as having a moral value, in other words as being moral, and whatever does not comply will be judged as not having a moral value, in other words as being immoral. The concept pair of good and evil is only the tautological expression of this fact. The same observation applies to the distinctions, which correspond to the sphere of economy, between something that has economic value and something that does not, between the economical and the non-economical. We can of course extend a more special scope to all of these distinctions, to use in particular spheres of life: we can thus, in the sphere of the aesthetic, name a particular form of value "graceful", another "majestic", and their nonaesthetic opposite forms "ungraceful" and "insignificant". Similarly, in the sphere of morality, the final distinctions of good and evil can correspond to the particular distinctions of the proper and the improper, of the noble and the vulgar. Also in the sphere of the economic, we can establish within the final distinctions between the economic and the noneconomic the particular distinctions between the useful and the harmful, the good and the bad yield. But none of these particular distinctions contain, either, any indication which would permit the determination of the specific content of each of these spheres of life in question for they are also only the tautological expression of the concepts to determine.

Owing to the tautological nature of all these final distinctions, it is not at all difficult to establish those which correspond to the sphere of the political. Just as we can establish through simple logical deduction, starting from the meaning of the word "morality" or the word "aesthetic", the final distinctions between that which has a moral value and that which does not, or between that which has an aesthetic value and that which does not, we can similarly, from the concept of the political, logically deduce the final distinction between that which has a political value and that which does not, between the political and the nonpolitical.

The sole difference is here in the terminology. While we have created special terms to designate the final distinctions of good and evil, of beautiful and ugly, of economic and noneconomic in the spheres of morality, aesthetics or economics, which have been the object of methodical analysis for centuries, the sphere of the political does not possess such special terms for its final distinctions. These special distinctions only weigh in within political values which already possess more concrete content. They then express a certain degree of value from the point of view of the concept of the political as determined by its content. From this point of view, we can distinguish, for example, the exercise of supremacy, considered to be politically of value (political), from the passive acceptance of supremacy, considered to be politically without value (nonpolitical). It is clear that the distinction between friend and foe corresponds neither to the final distinctions which have been in question, nor to their primary concrete derivatives. For the friend–foe concept pair in no way results from the concept of the political with the same logical necessity as that which permits one to deduce, from the concepts of morality, of aesthetics or of economy, the pairs consisting of:

- morally worthy, moral, good – morally unworthy, immoral, bad; or
- aesthetically worthy, aesthetic, beautiful – aesthetically unworthy, nonaesthetic, ugly; or also
- economically worthy, economic, practical – economically unworthy, noneconomic, impractical.

Let us now compare in parallel the friend–foe pair with those more concrete forms consisting of the fundamental distinctions which we have observed above, such as, for example, the pairs of good and bad yield, of graceful and awkward, or even, in the political system, of exercise and of passive acceptance of supremacy. It thus immediately becomes apparent that the friend–foe pair corresponds to a much more advanced degree of specialization, which would make it the equivalent, in the moral system, of the specialized pair of "saint–sinner", in the economic system of "thrifty father–spend-thrift father", or, in the political system itself, of the antithetical pair of great statesman and of indifferent petit bourgeois. But here also, when analyzing the logical structure of all these concept pairs which represent an equal degree of specialization, we find that the logical structure of the friend–foe pair is radically different from that of the other pairs of the same degree taken from the spheres of morality, economy, or politics.

These last pairs in fact only realize, to a certain degree of intensity, the fundamental distinctions of the spheres to which they belong: the pious man is the one who realizes what is morally of value, the sinner is the one who realizes what is morally without value, the thrifty family man realizes what is economically worthy, the spend-thrift what is not economically worthy. They thus all represent the values in question to a certain degree and in a certain form of their realization. But could we assert in the same way that the foe represents what is politically without value, while the friend represents what is politically of value? The answer is obviously no. From the point of view of the distinctions which directly result from the concept of the political, the foe can equally be of political value as politically without value, and the same can be said for the friend, according to whether one or the other corresponds or does not correspond to the ideas of value contained in the concept of the political. Thus, not only does the determination of fundamental categories, in the way that they were conceived of by Schmitt, lead in fact to a tautological expression of the meaning of the fundamental concepts, but in addition, the distinction proposed by him between friend and foe does not correspond to any of these fundamental categories and could not be derived from them.

The distinction between friend and foe derives from a wholly different sphere, and if Schmitt has been able to place it on the same logical plain as the fundamental distinctions of the categories of good and evil, of beautiful and ugly etc. – all the while admitting that it did not have the same scope – and if he has been able to attribute to it, in the sphere of the political, the same function as that of these various categories in their respective spheres, it is by giving the impression that both cases are in fact the result of the same logical operation. However, while these last categories establish, as we have seen, some abstract distinctions within an objectively determined value sphere, and that afterwards, a judgment based on these categories establishes a logical link between a life phenomenon and an abstract value, such as "the moral", "the political" or "the aesthetic", the friend–foe concept pair on the other hand, as much as it is conceived according to the value spheres in question, expresses a distinction within a value sphere which is determined individually, thus within the political sphere of a certain individual or of a certain group of individuals. In this case, it expresses a factual connection between the concrete political goals attributed to this individual or this group of individuals and one person, group of people or qualified object psychologically linked to the goals in question.

The links of friendship and enmity constitute independent sociological phenomena which have at their basis a determinate psychological attitude. The term "friend" designates a person (or a group of people or a personified object, respectively) of which the psychological connection towards another person and their life sphere is of a positive nature, meaning which is favorable to them; on the other hand, the "foe" is a person (or a group of people or a personified object, respectively) of which the psychological connection toward another person is of a negative nature, meaning which is not favorable to them. This connection will not remain as a rule within the confines of the sphere of interior life – it will not remain "platonic" – rather, it will tend to manifest itself in the outside world in some sort of objective form. The subject of this connection will thus strive to "testify" to it by some sort of expression of their thoughts and feelings, or by their actions, and they will do so according to the nature of this connection, either in a way favorable to the person in question and to his or her political goals, or in a way which is not favorable to them.

The political friend will thus be the person who promotes or seeks to promote the political goals pursued by another person, or who is at least willing to do so. The political foe will be the person who impedes or who seeks to impede the realization of these goals. Similarly, the artistic friend will be the one who facilitates the realization of the artist's aesthetic goals, and the foe the one who hinders them. Thus again, the commercial friend will be the one who helps or who is willing to help a person in the professional realization of their economic goals, and the commercial foe, particularly the competitor, will be the one who prevents or who is ready to prevent the realization of these goals. Finally, the friend of a given moral movement will be the one who seeks to bring it closer to reaching its goals, while the foe will oppose them or be ready to oppose them.

What must we understand therefore by the fact of distinguishing between friend and foe, in these various spheres and from the point of view of the fundamental categories which derive from them? The existence of a friend signifies a real or latent progress from the point of view of the realization of the values expressed by the concept, for there exists in all cases a favorable state of mind, a "friendly" state of mind, a certain "disposition" to promote it. Conversely, the existence of a foe signifies a real or at least latent obstacle from the point of view of the realization of the goals in question, for there exists in all cases a "hostile" state of mind, a certain "disposition" to hinder it. Thus the one who distinguishes between friend and foe while pursuing political, moral, aesthetic or economic goals also establishes a distinction between what tends to promote the realization of his or her goal and what tends to hinder it.

However, although it is not the case for all the other spheres, an ambiguity can arise in the political sphere – and only there – from the fact that certain terms receive in this sphere a double meaning. For the concept pair "politically of value, political – politically without value, nonpolitical" does not solely apply to an abstract distinction of the phenomena from the point of view of their belonging or of their not belonging to the political sphere, but it also serves to distinguish between the facts which tend to promote the realization of the particular values of this sphere and the facts which tend to hinder this realization. When we say, for example, that the banning of a newspaper is "politically without value" or "nonpolitical", in no way do we intend by that statement to formulate a general judgment that the ban of a newspaper would not enter, as such, in the sphere of political values. We limit ourselves to asserting that this ban is not meant, in this given case, to help reach the political goal which is being pursued, that it is without value for the realization of the political goal, that it is without value for such and such a policy. Similarly, if we were to say that China is to Yugoslavia "without political value," we would not understand by this that the Chinese state does not constitute as such a political value, but only that from the point of view of the realization of the political goals of Yugoslavia, China does not at present play any role, that it is "without value for the current concrete policy of Yugoslavia." This ambiguity of terms comes from the fact that the distinction between on the one hand "politically of value or political", and on the other hand "politically without value or non-political" was made by us from the point of view of a concept of the "political" considered as a distinct sphere independent from other value spheres (aesthetic etc.). According to the language of "the political" in the sense of the art of politics, however, we understand that "politically of value", (i.e., "political") means that which has value for the realization of a concrete political goal, and that "politically without value", (i.e., "nonpolitical") means that which is without value for the realization of this goal. It is mostly in the latter sense that the concept and the distinction in question have been used during the 19th century.

One very general observation will help further bring to light our point of view: the distinction between friend and foe could not have any logical link whatsoever with the judgments stemming from the fundamental categories which we have considered (with the exception of a single case which we will explore). These categories allow us to establish, on account of the value determinations which they in fact contain, whether a given phenomenon constitutes a moral, economic, aesthetic, or political value, and thus whether it can serve as a goal to moral, economic, aesthetic, or political activities. But from the point of view of all of these values, the distinction between friend and foe retains an absolutely neutral character. It relates only, within each of these spheres, to the conditions necessary for the realization of the values in question; and conversely, the distinctions made on the basis of the fundamental categories remain completely independent from the distinction between friend and foe. Thus the conditions which could be necessary, in a given case, to the realization of an aesthetic value could just as well be, in themselves, without aesthetic value; and the conditions which could eventually be necessary to the realization of a political value must not necessarily themselves have political value. In the sphere of art, there are ugly patrons, and in the sphere of politics, there are quite nonpolitical friends. A condition favorable to the realization of a moral goal can in itself be immoral. The principle according to which "the end justifies the means" serves only to translate this observation by limiting it to the conditions created by the person who is acting herself (i.e., to the means). In addition, it implies the will to morally justify the recourse to the means in question.

This rule, as we have seen, brooks one exception. The distinction between friend and foe being only the personification of the distinction between the conditions likely to promote the realization of a specific goal and those likely to hinder it, is reduced in the final analysis to a distinction of an economic nature. Indeed, to a more advanced degree of concrete expression and personification, it is a product of the economic category "useful and harmful", only no longer conceived of in a state of effective realization, but in a latent state. The distinction between the useful and the harmful is but a judgment on the connection between a given condition and a given goal, and the pursuit of the condition necessary to the realization of a given goal constitutes the economic problem *par excellence*. Just as political character does not belong by logical necessity to a certain constant number of facts falling within the political sphere because of their very nature, economic character, according to the common meaning of the word can just as well be present in all the other spheres of human activity. Thus in the economic sphere, the distinction between the economic friend and foe is identical to the distinction which derives, to a certain degree of concrete expression and personification, from the fundamental category of the economic itself. For the fundamental category of this sphere, that of the useful and the harmful, does not express anything but the distinction between the conditions likely to promote or hinder the realization of a specific goal. And we have seen that the distinction between friend and foe is nothing but a personification of this distinction broadened to the sphere of latent possibilities.[28]

The distinction between friend and foe still retains this meaning when it is directly applied to the fundamental categories themselves or to their derivatives, thus when we state that evil is the enemy of the good, the ugly the enemy of the beautiful etc. In this case we consider that the realization in the world of an absolute beauty, or an absolute good, is a moral or aesthetic goal the achievement of which comes up against the inevitable existence of evil or ugliness, which thus play the role of a hindrance or of a "foe." The fundamental categories of evil or ugly here themselves become the object of the personified distinction between the useful and the harmful. Lucifer is in this sense the "foe of the Lord", foolishness is the "foe of reason", the spiritual is the "foe of the worldly."

The distinction between friend and foe, moreover, does not have, in the political sphere, an absolute nature – we will come back to this point, which we limit ourselves solely to mentioning for now, in the ulterior work which we have previously alluded to: it is not a given once and for all and is not necessarily attached, as such, to the concept itself of certain specific objects. On the contrary, it is relative, just like any condition is always relative to the goal being pursued.[29] In the spheres which we have considered, there do not exist any "constitutional" enmities, just as there are no friendships which are of an "eternal" nature. Certain conditions can be useful for the realization of a specific goal, but can be harmful for the realization of another. The sturdiest political friendship can morph into enmity, and vice versa, as soon as the economic connection between its object and the goal being pursued is modified, or when this goal itself changes. When a foe is completely vanquished, even down to his spirit, the enmity vanishes, for the foe completely forswears inhibiting the political goals of the victor. Yesterday's foe being no longer harmful, nor even disposed to being so, he is no longer a "foe." And even, when the political goal consists in or manifests itself in reducing the vanquished to total helplessness, internal as well as external, the vanquished foe can, by morally submitting to his own helplessness, promote the realization of the political goal of the victor and thus become a friend. This is what Homer meant to say when he put these unusual words into the mouth of Achilles as he prepares to kill a vanquished Lycaon: "Die then, my friend!"[30]

In no way do we intend to contest the importance of the friend–foe connection for the determination of the content of the political sphere, and we do not in particular presume that this connection's role as an independent sociological phenomenon limits itself to the function which it fulfills within the various value spheres. We have only wished to establish that the determination of fundamental categories such as Schmitt's is not scientifically of great use for the definition of the content of the political and for its delimitation from the other value spheres and that, in addition, the distinction between friend and foe is neither a fundamental distinction of this sort, nor one of its derivatives. On the contrary, as a functional element common to all these value spheres, it possesses a radically different logical structure which could not in any way be compared to that of the fundamental categories. We will thus keep to this observation (which, it seems, is likely to weaken the logical foundations of Schmitt's political metaphysics) and return to the consideration of the characteristics of the concept of the political and its content, which we have already sketched out.

The observations we have been able to make in the sphere of human life in general find their verification in the sphere of the life of states, and, in particular, in the sphere of their external life which is especially of interest to us here.

All foreign policy is only the will to maintain, increase or assert one's power (*puissance*), and these three manifestations of political will are expressed here by the fundamental empirical forms consisting of: the policy of the status quo, the imperialist policy, and the policy of prestige. Here again, it is as a general rule an objective value, which is to say a universally recognized one, which attaches itself to the objects of the two first forms of foreign policy, while the object of the policy of prestige distinguishes itself by the disproportion existing between the objective value which is commonly attributed to it and the intensity of the political will which is related to it. To justify a policy of imperialist expansion the state will also invoke the superiority in relation to the state which will be the object of this policy, of its own qualities and of its own needs, which will always be in relation to the object of this policy.

However, this concept of the political in the literal sense takes on an aspect which is particular to it on two points. While in common parlance the concept of the political assumes, as one of its important elements, that considerable intellectual means are implemented to reach the political goal being pursued, this element plays a much smaller role in the concept of the political in the literal sense. For any state activity pursuing a goal of power is qualified as political even when it does not involve the implementation of considerable intellectual means. Otherwise, the sphere of the political in the literal sense would no doubt appear drastically reduced. However, the opposition to the use of physical force remains here intact, at least when it comes to organized physical force: we will not be able to speak of politics here either if, to reach the sought-after political goal, the state resorts to organized physical force. This is what Clausewitz states: "War is a mere continuation of policy by other means."[31] The goal of war is, like that of policy, power, but the means which it uses are not policy's own.

In addition, the concept of the political takes on, when applied to the sphere of the state, two different meanings from a qualitative point of view. Sometimes it globally designates the activity of the state aiming to maintain, increase or assert its power in specific spheres, and, from this point of view, according to whether it concerns the sphere of trade, of colonies or of a particular region of the world, for example the Mediterranean, we will then speak of commercial, colonial or Mediterranean policy. Sometimes we can distinguish within the whole group of possible foreign activity spheres of the state certain particular spheres, and within the whole group of state activity certain particular modes of this activity which we then designate as political matters and political activities in the particular sense of the word, as qualified political matters and activities. Stemming this time from the definition of the content of the concept of the political, we thus find ourselves confronted by the same necessity that had already been apparent to us when we considered this concept solely from the purely formal point of view of the connection between the subject of the concept of the political, which is the state, and its various objects: the necessity of establishing a qualitative differentiation between two distinct notions of the political.

The political taken in the general sense being the will of the state to maintain, increase or assert its power, this element of the will to power must appear in the concept of the qualified political which is also sometimes called "high politics" in a more qualified manner and to a much stronger degree. The political object in the particular sense will be, thereafter, the object which is in the mind of the state deploying a political activity, especially likely to satisfy its will to power. The political activity in the literal sense will thus be the activity which relates to objects of this nature and in which the state's will to power then manifests itself with a particular degree of intensity and clarity.

Because a given state makes certain objects into the preferred goal of its will to power and deploys towards them particularly significant activity, because it thus makes them into the preferred object of its will and of its activity, the state creates between it and these objects a particularly strong and intense connection. The concept of the political determined by its content thus results in confirming the concept which we had established by placing ourselves first from a *formal* point of view. We can thus say that *the political in the specific sense consists in the particular degree of intensity of the connection created by the state's will to power between its objects and the state.*

4
On the Concept of Political Disputes

It is now appropriate to ask ourselves a question of principle which is essential as much for the theory as for the practice of international law. What is the link which exists between this sphere of the political and the sphere of the international legal system? We will first limit ourselves to considering the two aspects of the political which express themselves by the will either to maintain or to increase one's power.[1]

Let us remind ourselves that we have already had the opportunity to mention, from a slightly different point of view, these two concepts of the maintenance and the increase of power, namely when we were discussing fundamental problems of which we were saying, at the beginning of this treatise (Chapter 1), that their solution is called for by any fully developed legal system. One of those problems we had mentioned was that of the delimitation of the different spheres of power and of their modifications. To the political will aiming to maintain power as well as to its various manifestations corresponds indeed in a fully developed legal system a system of norms which allow the determination, on the basis of objective criteria, of the limits of the spheres of power pertaining to this will. By legitimizing the objectification of this will within the limits thus determined, these norms create the conditions necessary to ensure the protection of these limits. And to the will aiming to increase power as well as to its manifestations corresponds, on the other hand, within a fully developed legal system a system of norms which fix the conditions and the limits to which the law subordinates any modification of the spheres of power. By legitimizing in this manner the modifications taking place within the framework of the conditions and limits they prescribe, these norms create the bases allowing the legal protection of the power modifications which take place in accordance with these conditions to be ensured. The static sphere of politics aiming to maintain power and the dynamic sphere of politics aiming to increase power would thus correspond, in the sphere of law, to a system of distributive static and dynamic norms.[2]

However, neither the domestic legal system nor even the international legal system corresponds fully to this outline. Because of the very nature of law, any legal system possesses a certain static tendency. The principles of order, rationality, and predictability, which are immanent to the nature of law and which all result from the principle of legal security, indeed require before all else the delimitation and the maintenance of the spheres of power (*pouvoir*) which the legal system is called upon to manage. From the point of view of these principles, considered in their consequences, any modification of existing power relations entails an element of unrest, of precarious order, of unpredictability, and of undeterminability, thus constituting an element of latent danger threatening the very existence of the legal system, a danger against which the system would have to defend itself in the name of the principles in question to ensure its existence. It is, however, quite obvious that no legal system could in the long run maintain itself if it purported to push these principles to their final consequences; for the tendency to the modification of the spheres of power also results from sociological necessities, just as does the tendency of the maintenance of the existing spheres of power. And if the legal system does not sufficiently take this tendency into account, it will seek to manifest itself against the law (*droit*), which would constitute a much more formidable danger for the maintenance of the legal system. This is why any legal system should include norms of a dynamic character, more or less articulate, which fix the conditions and the limits to which the modifications of the spheres of power will be subjected, and which, by determining these conditions, permit the objectivation of the political tendency aiming to increase power to realize itself in a predictable and prescribed way.

In particular, it is the goal of the domestic legal system to offer, within its sphere, an area where the struggle for the spheres of power (*puissance*) can continue without resorting to violence and where it is possible to determine the strongest through peaceful competition and by peaceful means as fixed by the state. To that end, the state must establish a system of values and of scales of all kinds, where the most diverse elements appear (such as money, administration positions available through competition, the possibilities offered by the parliamentary system), the possession of which symbolically represents the existing power (*pouvoir*) relationships between individuals. In order for any modification in the power (*force* [in the sense of *pouvoir*]) relationships between individuals to find adequate expression through an increase or a decrease in the possession of these values, the state should have recourse to a system of elastic norms likely to resist, without breaking, even the greatest pressures from the interests being grappled with, and the state ensures the effectiveness of these norms by completely concentrating in its hands the whole of the organized physical forces (*forces physiques*).[3]

In the history of the state's domestic life, it is only in exceptional cases that the elasticity of this system of norms, together with the concentration of the whole of the organized physical forces in the hands of the state, is no longer sufficient to convey within the framework of the law a simultaneous and homogeneous shift of forces among a considerable number of individuals. Under the pressure of mounting forces which can no longer find recognition in the system of norms sanctioned by the state, this system will then be shattered by an act of violence. This act is revolution and the situation which presents itself in the moment when the old system of norms is destroyed and a new system is not yet established, is anarchy.

No legal system could ever fully make room in its sphere for the political tendency towards increasing power (*puissance*). Between the static and the dynamic tendencies, each seeking to leave its mark on the internal conformation of the law, there exists an unsolvable antinomy which as a rule results in a more or less enduring sort of *modus vivendi* where the static element predominates. If we set aside even nature in a final static analysis of the law, there still exist two further reasons which will always ensure the supremacy of the static tendency: it is, on the one hand, the fact – which I propose to examine more closely in an ulterior study[4] – that the psychological phenomenon of a general nature which appears in political will has a marked tendency to expand disproportionally, exceeding all rational limits, and that, as a result, the unreserved acceptance of such

a tendency in a given legal system would inevitably lead, in its ultimate logical consequences, to the abolition of any system whatsoever and consequently to the negation of the very principles which
make up the essence of law (*droit*). And it is, furthermore, the fact
that social groups, the influence of which is decisive for the conformation of a given legal system, and which necessarily possess within
the community certain specific spheres of power (*pouvoir*), will
always strive to ensure, in the legal system subjected to their influence, the maintenance and the protection of the spheres of power
(*pouvoir*) in question.

International law in particular is in no position to even approximately achieve this task. For, other than the fact that there exists no
organized and monopolized physical force in the international sphere
susceptible to sanction the validity of international law, the development of this law has not gone beyond the point where is precisely
born the second of these fundamental functions of any legal system,
which we discussed in the beginning (Chapter 2). International law
has, certainly, created norms susceptible to establish a given state
of the law; but as for norms which would permit the modification
of a given state of law by peaceful means, even against the will of
the state that this modification would have an adverse effect upon,
these only exist in international law in a most rudimentary manner. It all depends on the point of the good will of the state concerned: we might as well say that it depends on random chance.[5] At
the current stage of its development, international law is of a clearly
static nature.[6] Regarding the mutual power (*force*) relations between
the various members of the international community and the corresponding needs determined by these relations, international law
limits itself to establishing a relationship which has existed in the
past at a specific moment in time between two given states, namely
at the moment when the existing state of law began, as well as establishing what needs were at that moment in time deemed worthy of
receiving recognition in the law. In international law, it is in the
modifications of the spheres of power (*puissance*) sometimes determined by diplomatic acts that a change in the power (*force*) relationship between two states can be expressed accidentally, indirectly,
and with generally very little clarity.

If in domestic law the evolution of the power (*force*) relationships
between individuals and the corresponding evolution of the state of

law happens in a uniform and continuous way, in international life, however, this evolution is achieved on different levels and following a varying rhythm. On the one hand, there is the evolution of the power (*force*) relationship between two states such as determined by the course of history; and above this evolution, on the other hand, there is the rigid coating of international law, uniformly immobile and fixed and which, being unable to yield to the pressures it is subjected to, must break when this pressure reaches a certain degree of intensity. The state which considers that a shift in forces has occurred to its advantage, in relation to the existing state of law, will then endeavor to resolve in the direction of the real power (*force*) relationship the discrepancy which exists, according to this state, between this real relationship and the legal situation corresponding to the previously existing power (*force*) relationship. This state will consequently strive to adapt the legal situation to what it considers to be the real power (*force*) relationship. Conversely, the state which finds that its sphere of influence threatens to be diminished by this tendency will strive to maintain the existing legal situation.[7]

In such cases, what are the various concrete goals pursued by states which oppose each other in such a way, apart from the general goal consisting in the increase or the maintenance of power (*puissance*)? And what are the specific forms taken by their opposition? These various concrete goals can be of two kinds: imperialist expansion can aim for, on the one hand, a concrete modification determined by mutual spheres of power (*puissance*), that is to say the acquisition of a power (*pouvoir*) which until then had belonged to another state. But this policy can also, on the other hand (and this is here probably the most common case) rest on the simple, general, non-differentiated feeling of a discrepancy between the legal situation and the real power (*force*) relationship. It will then only express itself through a general tendency aiming to the modification of the existing legal situation, a modification of which the goals will not be shared in advance and will only be specified as a rule on the basis of the new power (*force*) relationship resulting from the resolution of this discrepancy.[8]

Now, as for the forms which can take the opposition in question between two given states, we would be tempted to say that this opposition manifests itself precisely in the form of international disputes. But that is exactly where lies what we believe to be, for the theory of international disputes, the decisive problem. For international disputes manifest oppositions which express themselves in a clear and precise way through a demand which is formulated on the one hand and contested on the other. For an opposition to be able to manifest itself in the guise of a dispute, the object of the dispute must thus be rationally formulated and delineated; in other words, the parties involved must be in a position to make the dispute the object of a "discussion" and must be able to express their diverging points of view through arguments which are more or less clear and precise, in order to achieve some solution acceptable to both parties. But we have seen that international law does not possess, as in the manner of private law, an organized system of universally recognized values and of elastic norms which would permit the determination of the real power (*force*) relationship, as well as of the real needs, in an objective and indisputable way recognized as such by both parties. Such a system does not exist in the international community, even outside the sphere of positive international law.

For example, should State A consider that its development and its needs would justify its participation in naval supremacy and in the exploitation of colonies which until then were exclusively the reserve of State B, it could well express in a clear and precise way its desire to possess a part of State B's colonies, and the latter state could, for its part, express in a no less clear and precise way its opposition to such a desire. However, for there to be a dispute, there is still lacking one condition, namely some possibility of coming to a decision on the conflict between the two states on the basis of positive international law, or some other system of norms susceptible to general application. For, in a case of this sort, it is not a "right" that is asserted by State A and which can be contested by State B; the disagreement between states A and B does not relate to a question of positive international law, as State A itself recognizes that its desire does not rest on positive international law. It is not on positive law, on the law as it is in force, on which the parties would base themselves if they wished to give their diverging points of view the character of a dispute, but rather on justice: in other words from the point of view of A, on the law as it should be, and from the point of view of B, on the law, perfectly correct, as it is already realized. Such a divergence in views could only be the object of a discussion and take on the form of a dispute if two preliminary conditions were fulfilled. The first being that the object of the divergence of views (in the present case the claim to obtain colonies belonging to another state, clearly contrary to the arrangements of positive international law) must already have been subjected to a rational analysis which, by teasing out a system of objective concepts, would allow the undertaking of a discussion on this matter susceptible to result in a solution which could be objectively considered as obligatory. The second condition would be that the international community must have reached a level of development allowing the formation not only of common concepts of international law, but also of common concepts of justice which, even should they not yet be crystallized into legal norms, would nonetheless already permit a decision to be made on a divergence of views such as the one in question on the basis of norms susceptible to general application.

But neither the rational analysis condition nor the one requiring consent on the objective criteria of what is just are met in the community of states. Their absence removes any characteristic of a dispute from the opposition in question, and renders impossible its solution by third parties, even on the basis of equity. For, as has been previously pointed out,[9] a decision based on equity also assumes the existence of norms susceptible to general application, even though the dominant doctrine generally omits to take this into account. However, the rules susceptible to general application are solely those resting on a system of accomplished concepts of which the content, at least concerning the sphere of international relations, has received the approval of the members of the community.

The same is true, but in an even stronger measure, of the second of State A's desires, which aims for the inclusion of a sea into its sphere of influence which until then was subjected to State B's exclusive domination. Lacking here is not only the possibility of a discussion allowing the glimpse of an objectively obligatory solution for both parties, but also the possibility of a reasonable statement of opposing viewpoints. For example, could State A reasonably demand from State B that it force its fishermen to no longer enter the waters of a sea which, by virtue of international law, is unquestionably open to the nationals of State B, or that State B yield a part of its naval bases in this sea, or of its trade carried out on those sea routes? This is why disarmament and security problems cannot be solved through the means which diplomacy has heretofore seen fit to apply to them.

Where can be found rationally elaborated concepts susceptible to general application which would allow one to examine and to compare the needs of various states concerning security and the possession of military forces of a specific quantity and quality? And where then can be found a universally accepted and obligatory measure of values (banishing from the parties any notion of the arbitrary) which would allow one to rule on the legitimacy of the contradictory claims of the states?

This explains why concrete questions of security and disarmament have not yet been addressed.[10] The fundamental cause is found neither in some diplomatic tactic nor in the states' ill will, nor in the incompetence of their representatives, but solely in the impossibility of finding rational expression for the various points of view of the states which could become the object of discussion and an eventual agreement.[11]

Excursus: 'tension,' 'dispute,' and the concept of the political

There is no place for such conflicts in the sphere of international disputes, in other words for conflicts the object of which is precisely a modification of the spheres of power determined by positive international law. Located on the outside of the sphere of clear concepts, they form a separate sphere within interstate oppositions, with unique proprietary characteristics. It is a distinct category of interstate oppositions which has not yet become the object of a systematic study in legal science, and we propose to apply to them the term "tensions."[12] We understand by this term, by summarizing thus the result of our analysis in a brief formula, *those interstate oppositions which have as their object an existing discordance, according to the opinion of a given state, between the real powers (force) and the needs of this state on the one hand and the existing legal situation on the other.*[13] There thus exist two superimposed layers of international oppositions, two layers which correspond to each other up to a certain extent following the same vertical line: the first, clear and rational, distinctly perceived in the consciousness of peoples – this is the layer of disputes; and underneath it, a layer which does not yet come from rational regulation and the existence of which, apart from exceptional violent explosions, only manifests itself indirectly – these are the "tensions."

Underneath the international life, which is apparent in diplomatic and legal acts, these "tensions" live a generally latent life.

Our analysis results in the following: that as permanent elements of social life, these "tensions" do not constitute a special feature of interstate relations; they manifest themselves equally in the domestic life of the state, although under a different form and with different legal consequences. They are, by definition, of a political nature, and are only a particular manifestation of the political in that it opposes itself to the sphere of law. To the extent that political forces of a dynamic nature, which are at the base of these tensions, are not recognized in the international legal system, they will seek to realize themselves by other means: not directly, according to the means of the law, because the sphere of disputes is closed off to them, but through the means of indirect relations of a particular nature, with the sole form which allows interstate relations to be given legal expression, in other words with disputes. For, given that at the very least it is, for the state asserting a demand, in its best interest for the "tension" to be resolved in its favor, the state will endeavor to express it in a form susceptible to be recognized by the international community. The state has at its disposal for that purpose only one means, which is the dispute. The study of relations which can exist between tensions and disputes will bring us one conclusive step closer, we believe, towards a scientifically correct classification of international disputes.

It can happen that a dispute exists between two states without there being a tension at the same time, or that despite the simultaneous existence of a tension, a dispute is by no means influenced by it. Such disputes lead an absolutely independent existence and draw their own significance solely from themselves. We shall call them "pure disputes."

Here is an example of such a dispute: between states A and B there exists a tension which relates to the immigration ban decreed by State A against State B's nationals; and there exists at the same time, between these same states, a dispute concerning the interpretation of a monetary convention, without either of these states establishing any link whatsoever between this dispute and the tension. These two layers of disputes and tensions will not necessarily remain without links to one another; they can even mutually influence each other. The sphere of disputes can only act on the sphere of tensions in one way, in that a tension can be transferred, wholly or partially, to the category of disputes, or in other words that the object of the tension, having been rationally conceived, has been able to be integrated into the sphere of norms susceptible to general application. If the tension has been able to be wholly absorbed into the sphere of disputes, it has in this case become a dispute itself, and the tension *per se* no longer exists. The opposition which has in such a way become a dispute no longer possesses in itself a political nature.

Example: Let us suppose that in the case we have just examined the matter of immigration into State A of State B nationals has become the object, in all its aspects, of a rational analysis. At the same time, a community of views is established between states A and B on the basis of a common concept of what is just regarding the immigration problem. The opposition between these two states will have thus lost the nature of a tension and will be susceptible, at the same time as it is rationally formulated, to be decided on the basis of norms for general application; in other words, this opposition will have acquired the nature of a dispute.

The situation presents itself differently when the tension is only partially integrated into the sphere of disputes, in such a way that a part of the tension becomes a dispute and the other part remains a tension. The object of the dispute then resurfaces in the same complex of issues which gave rise to the tension. But the dispute in this case will only encompass the most advanced ramifications of the tension, those which in a way already penetrate into the layer of the legal system, while the body of the tension, strictly speaking, according to our definition, remains beyond this layer. Disputes which are found to be, compared with a tension, in a relationship of this sort could be called "disputes with overflowing tensions."

Example: In our last case, the tension between states A and B lingers. Its object has simply shrunk, in the sense that a treaty has been concluded between the two states regulating the formation of commercial corporations established by B's nationals on State A's territory. In this way, disputes could from now on occur on matters which before would have been part of the object of the tension. A dispute born from the interpretation of this treaty would in a way encompass an advanced ramification of the tension which, in all other ways, lingers.

It is completely different when the influence exerted by the sphere of tensions on that of disputes is considered; here we touch on the vital point of the problem we are studying. If the purely legal content of the dispute and its purely objective elements were not subject to the effects of the tension, its specific nature, however, its scope and its tone are necessarily modified under the pressure of the tension, seeking a way out through the rigid coating of the relationship governed by the law. The agitation which manifests itself at the base of interstate relations is communicated to the layers superimposed to it, where, as an after-effect, these relationships lose their friendly and peaceful nature. The tension, which due to the absence of a consensus on the regulatory principles potentially applicable to it, and owing to the insufficient development of the logical analysis, finds no access to the sphere of disputes, undergoes a "repression" (to borrow an image in favor in modern psychology): it can only manifest itself by proxy through disputes, and it will use to this effect disputes of which the object happens to have some link with what could be called the concrete content of the tension.

This is why "disputes with overflowing tensions" necessarily take on a political nature. In the case which we have imagined, the intensity of the connection existing between State A and the immigration problem which is the object of the tension is reflected onto the issue of immigration *per se*. For this matter is part as such of the will to power (*puissance*) of the state, in other words, of its political activity, and the intensity which is peculiar to it extends in an undivided way to the issue as a whole. Due to the relationship existing between the object of the dispute and that of the tension, the state considers both of these objects as being at least of a very similar value, of constituting a unit of some sort. For due to this relationship, a decision concerning the dispute implies at the same time a partial decision on the object of the tension. This is why the state reacts with particular intensity to those issues, which are the object of these two kinds of opposition, and thus bestows upon them a political characteristic.

However, given that, as we have seen, a tension does not always possess a concrete object and that, moreover, a tension possessing a concrete object is not always partially integrated into the sphere of disputes, the tension will very often have to resort by proxy to other disputes. These disputes will thus have no relationship whatsoever with the more or less concrete object of the tension, which, for its part, will have no access to the sphere of disputes. In such a case, there will be thus no way to establish a relationship of an objective nature between the tension and the dispute. This relationship thus will be only of a subjective nature, meaning that the dispute will appear as the representative or the substitute of the tension. The dispute will have as its object an issue completely alien to the concrete opposition which would be in a way the expression of the tension. The dispute will have here the appearance of a pure dispute, but will not be so in reality. Disputes which are found to be in a relationship of this sort, with regards to a tension, could be called "disputes with representative functions" or "virtually pure disputes."[14]

Example: In the case which we have considered, the tension relating to the immigration problem lingers. At the same time, there exists between states A and B a dispute concerning the interpretation of a monetary convention. State B, which sees no way, on the playing field of the tension, to force the recognition of the superiority (according to itself) of its own qualities and needs, substitutes in its political objectives this dispute to the tension and endeavors at all costs, by asserting its superiority with regard at least to this dispute, to indirectly manifest in this way superiority of a general nature.

What is then, we ask ourselves, the characteristic which alone will render a tension susceptible and worthy to be "represented" in this manner? It is the connection of the tension to the state, the place which it merits within the system of foreign policy goals recognized by the state. For this is here a character which, owing to its formal nature, can be transferred without any difference to magnitudes of a completely different objective kind. The importance of this characteristic lies in the fact that it is the intensity of the connection of a given object to the state on which the energy and activity of the state relating to the object in question depends. However, the intensity of this connection and the energy of the activity which results from it find themselves to be as great as possible in the sphere of tensions. For, as we have seen, in the mind of the states which are party to the tension, the place which the states will occupy within the international community directly depends on the solution given to a tension. By conferring on a dispute the place which should be occupied by a tension according to the hierarchy of its political objectives, the state concentrates on this dispute the will which it had in vain sought to assert on the playing field of the tension. Taking it as the symbol of the tension, the state turns its attention to this dispute with the same intensity which it would have brought to the tension and it endeavors in this indirect way to resolve the tension to its advantage. For in such a case, the solution of the dispute to the state's advantage takes on the value of a symbolic confirmation of the superior qualities which the state attributes to itself and which it seeks to prove.

By seeking to attribute to a given dispute a scope exceeding its legal object, the state attempts to obtain (by the solution of this dispute) the solution to the problem of its general position within the international community and thereby the solution to the tension. The state will thus transfer to a dispute of this nature all the forces of its will, and will implement, in order to resolve it, all its energy.

5
Conclusion

The scientific value of a theory can be judged from two different points of view. On the one hand, we can ask ourselves whether or not it agrees with the facts as a whole; facts to which it presumes to give a scientific systematization, and also whether it does not enclose in itself some contradiction. Any theory must be subjected to scrutiny of this sort. On the other hand, however, we can also ask ourselves, setting aside a theory's logical correctness and empirical truth, what *value* a theory can have for academia and for practice, and what interest its conclusions can have. It is only possible to subject a given theory to such scrutiny after having attempted, using this theory, to solve in a satisfying manner, or to bring closer to a satisfying conclusion, problems which until then could not be solved or which could only be insufficiently solved.

In the book which we had mentioned above,[1] we had endeavored to determine the limits of international jurisdiction by basing ourselves on the essential principles of present theory and to analyze the legal function of the *rebus sic stantibus* clause, at least in a general manner. We had come to the conclusion that the bodies of international jurisdiction are in a position to make an objective decision, whatever the nature or the content of the submitted claim. In other words, the possibility for an international judge to render objective decisions is in fact unlimited. However, we had established a distinction between this objective justiciability and subjective justiciability, meaning the possibility, *for the parties*, to submit the disputes which divide them to the decision of an international legal body. We had expressed the idea that the parties *are not in a position to* submit *political* disputes, in the sense which was defined in this study, to the decision of an international legal body, even though these disputes could in themselves be susceptible to a legal solution. For the international legal body would then have to adjudicate, in addition to the dispute, the tension which is at the base of the dispute, and the body does not possess norms susceptible to general application with which to make such a decision. Of course, it cannot be denied that a political dispute, precisely because of the fact that it finds itself submitted to a body of international jurisdiction, can be dispossessed of its political nature in certain cases, notably when it concerns a dispute with representative functions. It can be in a way "depoliticized," or in other words, dispossessed of its relationship to a tension. And, in fact, a number of disputes of an indisputably political nature, such as, not exactly the Alabama affair, but the Wimbledon case, or the dispute regarding a joint Austro-German customs project, or also various Polish-German disputes, have indeed been dispossessed of their political character by bodies of international jurisdiction. It would thus be preferable, instead of denying the subjective justiciability of all political disputes taken as a whole, to limit this concept to one part (which it is not possible to delineate more precisely) of political disputes, and to speak for the rest only of a psychological repugnance which states express at the idea of submitting political disputes to bodies of international jurisdiction. Scientific critiques have preoccupied themselves much less, it seems to us, with the theoretical foundations of our concept than with the juridico-political consequences which we had deduced from it. We have thus been able to set aside the arguments which scientific critiques had asserted, having precisely outlined our old theory in a new way as well as having gone into more detail with it.

Lauterpacht himself, who is perhaps the one which has given the most attention to our theory, considers the problem of the classification of international disputes mostly from the angle of their justiciability. It is certainly one of its most important aspects, the study of which constitutes one of the most serious tasks of international law, but the solution to this problem presupposes the previous existence of a scientifically unassailable classification of international disputes. It is solely this last purely theoretical task which has been the object of this present study. It has seemed to us all the more recommended and necessary to devote a monographic study to this matter (while setting aside all the particular problems which depend upon it) particularly as the solution to this question is not only susceptible to giving us a basis for the determination of the limits of international jurisdiction, but as it can in addition take on a decisive importance for the problems of the *clausula rebus sic stantibus*, of the "domaine réservé", of sovereignty, and of the interpretation of the Covenant of the League of Nations in general. We would even be ready to believe that the problem and the concept of the political could, beyond these particular matters, provide new clarity on the system of international law and of public law in general.

Notes

Preface

1. German and French titles from the main body of the text are immediately translated into English; their original versions are provided in individual footnotes, inserted by the editors, throughout the text; here: *Die internationale Rechtspflege, ihr Wesen und ihre Grenzen*, Leipzig, 1929 (the translator/editors).

1 Introduction

1. Here, and in the following, the italic terms in brackets indicate the French terminology of the original text (the translator/editors).
2. On this subject, see Burckhardt (1927); von Hippel (1930); Scelle (1932); Nelson (1924); Stammler (1911); see also Ulpian: *"Iuris praecepta sunt haec: honeste vivere, alterum non laedere, suum cuique tribuere"*. Note by the editors: here Morgenthau refers to the late Roman jurist Gnaeus Domitius Annius Ulpianus (170–223BC) from his *Digesta 1.1.10* which would be in English: *There are three principles of law – to live honorably, to harm no one, and to give to each his own* (the translator/editors).
3. We assume that this note relates to his *Habilitation* thesis on *"The Reality of International Legal Norms"*, published as *La réalité des normes. En particulier des normes du droit international*, Paris 1934 (the editors).

2 On the Concept of Legal Disputes

1. Thus Nippold (1907); Huber (1908); Marshall-Brown and Politis (1922); Hostie (1928); Verzijl (1925); Le Fur (1931); Politis (1924).
2. See Article 36 of the Hague Convention; Article 13, paragraph 2 of the Covenant of the League of Nations; Article 36 of the Statute of the Permanent Court of International Justice.
3. The original French version puts this sentence also in inverted commas; Morgenthau, however, gives no reference (the translator/editors).
4. Strisower (1919), also (1922); Schindler (1927); Kaufmann (1932).
5. Castberg (1925).
6. See Ray (1930); Decencière-Ferrandière (1929); Lauterpacht (1930).
7. It is appropriate to reject Mulder's formulation according to which one could not refer to the opinion of the parties, for the following reason: in this case, one would risk distorting the concept of the legal dispute by putting it in opposition to disputes in which, the claim being ill-founded in law, the

tribunal should, according to Mulder's interpretation, abandon the idea of receiving the claim and doing justice to the defender, for reasons of failure of jurisdiction. The opposite is true: the requirement of a legal motivation in no way signifies that this motivation must be grounded in law, with the result that the arbitral tribunal must allow this claim; the requirement simply means that the claim must invoke legal motives, whether they be grounded or not. The concept of the legal dispute thus does not oppose itself, in this formulation, to badly motivated legal disputes, but to disputes in which the claim disregards any legal argument, whatever it may be. By virtue of such a temporary definition of the legal dispute, identical in its foundation to the definition criticized by Mulder, the international legal bodies would be obligated to make a material decision in any case in which the claim, however poorly grounded it may be, will have invoked legal arguments. These bodies would declare themselves to be in failure of jurisdiction solely in the cases where the claim is not grounded on any legal argument, but is solely motivated by considerations alien to the law. – Note by the translator/ editors: Morgenthau refers here probably to B. Mulder, but gives, however, no bibliographical details; also no appropriate bibliographical details can be reconstructed. There is an article by B. Mulder – from 1926 – which is quite often referred to in the legal debates of the 1920s and 30s – Mulder, "Les lacunes du droit international public", *VII Revue de droit international et de législation comparée* – but this reference cannot be found in Morgenthau.

8. It is appropriate to rule out, for the same reason, the definition according to which legal disputes are disputes "about which the Parties are mutually contesting a right" – a definition which is contained in the agreements of Locarno and in the General Act for the Settlement of International disputes dated September 26, 1928, Articles 17 and 21; against this formulation, see also Decencière-Ferrandière (1929); in favor of this formulation see Verdross (1926).

9. This reference cannot be reconstructed.

10. Verzijl (1925, p. 743); also Hostie (1928); Redslob (1927); Schücking and Wehberg (1924).

11. The general principles of reason can only lend themselves to this if they are transposed in a way which is adapted to the particular subject of the various sciences, and the task of these sciences is precisely to formulate the rules which are specific to each of them while conforming to the general principles of reason, in other words to translate these principles into specific rules. Thus, in making the principles of reason intervene in a scientific definition, we pay no heed to what constitutes the essential task of scientific endeavor.

12. See amongst others Lord Phillimore (1921); also the Treaty of Arbitration between Brazil and Chile of 1899.

13. Ray (1930, p. 424); Guggenheim (1932); Barandon (1933).

14. This reference relates to Morgenthau's PhD dissertation "International Judicature"; see above note 1 under "Preface" (the editors).

15. See Lauterpacht (1930, pp. 640, 649).

3 The Concept of the Political

1. That this definition of the concept also encompasses the sphere of domestic politics results necessarily from the fact that foreign and domestic politics are not two spheres of a different nature, but only two different spheres to which applies one and the same principle, namely the political principle; see Smend (1923, 1928); Triepel (1923).
2. Thus Lauterpacht (1930, p. 564); Decencière-Ferrandière (1929, p. 427).
3. That is, the First World War (the editors).
4. Morgenthau argues here that in modern international law there is no codified prerogative right of one state over another state in the sense of exclusive rights or privileges held by certain states over other states as in domestic politics – for example, the president over other constitutional powers (the editors).
5. See Schindler (1927); Barandon (1933, p. 202); Gallus (1930, p. 225); Decencière-Ferrandière (1929, p. 417); Le Fur (1931, p. 472); see likewise Dimitch (1930, p. 48).
6. Quoted from Büchi (1914, pp. 64, 69); Lammasch (1912, p. 102).
7. Lauterpacht (1930, p. 576).
8. See the following excellent arguments against this draft and the fundamental ideas at its base: Strupp (1918, p. 69); Wehberg (1911, p. 63); Nippold (1908).
9. There should be an exception made here only in the case where it is the existence of the state as such which would constitute the subject of a matter. The political character of such a matter would then necessarily result from the nature of its subject. Indeed, a matter for which the solution depends on the very existence of the state could obviously not be more related to the state. However, this would be the most extreme of all cases, and it would be difficult to find many examples of this in practice. Besides, this matter would more or less never present itself in the form of a dispute between states. This is why we have not taken such a case into account in our study thus far, and why we can continue to ignore it.
10. See namely Wehberg (1911, pp. 50, 63); Fauchille (1921, p. 545); Schumpeter (1919, p. 3722); Strupp (1914; also 1918, p. 66; also 1932, p. 237); Nippold (1907, 1908); Marshall-Brown and Politis (1922); Meinecke (1925, p. 21); Scelle (1919, pp. 66, 67, 171); Hoijer (1926, pp. 227, 264); Huber (1908, p. 525); Borchard (1924, p. 53).
11. See Triepel (1918, p. 17); Schücking (1918, p. 52); Mariotte (1926, pp. 116, 119); Borchard (1924, p. 53); Vattel (1758, §332).
12. This concept of the "political" (inverted commas in the original; the translator), which did not originally feature in the article of Carl Schmitt "Der Begriff des Politischen", *Archiv für Sozialwissenschaft und Sozialpolitik*, 1927, was introduced by him in the reprint of this article, published separately under the same title in 1932. We find it since in the following writings of the same author: *Staatsethik und pluralistischer Staat*, Berlin, 1930; *Der Hüter der Verfassung*, Tübingen, 1931; and espe-

cially *Hugo Preuss, sein Staatsbegriff und seine Stellung in der deutschen Staatslehre*, Tübingen, 1930.

13. See Mariotte (1926, p. 117); Triepel (1918, p. 17); and the following Wehberg (1912, p. 92); Marshall-Brown and Politis (1922); Rousseau (1927, p. 202).

14. In a later writing – "Power as a Political Concept" (1971) – Morgenthau terms this "feeling" also "political wisdom" in reference to Aristotle (the editors).

15. In the French original text, Morgenthau writes, as indicated above, *loi*; to translate this with the English term "law" – as Morgenthau used the English "law" himself (see, for example, his "Six Principles of Political Realism"; as well as above in the editors' Introduction, Section 3) – would be, however, completely misleading, because Morgenthau seems to have something very different in mind than that which our modern intellect is inclined to associate with "law", namely fixed and eternal regularities of some natural or cosmic origin or something of like character. Indeed, however, Morgenthau seems to propose very differently a spatiotemporal contingent understanding of the term "law" which was typical for pre-modern, pre-positivist political thought, as, for example, in Charles de Montesquieu when he speaks of l'*esprit* des lois; see also Michel Bastit, *La naissance de la loi moderne*, Paris 1990 (the editors).

16. Thus Le Fur (1931, p. 472); Strupp (1929, pp. 68–9, note 1); also Strupp (1932, p. 237).

17. Morgenthau's reference cannot be identified here (the editors).

18. Morgenthau's reference cannot be identified here (the editors).

19. This reference of Morgenthau to Schindler is not identified in the original text with clear bibliographical details (the editors).

20. See Marshall-Brown and Politis (1922).

21. Morgenthau refers here to the *Institut de Droit International* (Institute of International Law) which was founded on September 8, 1873 in the Ghent Town Hall in Brussels. The Institute is an international consortium of leading international lawyers and was awarded the Nobel Peace Prize in 1904 in recognition of its action in favor of arbitration among states as a peaceful means of settling disputes. For further information see the Institute's webpage at http://www.idi-iil.org (the editors).

22. See Wehberg (1911, 1912); Politics (1922).

23. Thus the report of Borel and Politis (1922).

24. Against this resolution, see Fauchille (1921, p. 556), in favor of it Le Fur (1931, p. 472).

25. It is unclear here to which work of Croce Morgenthau refers (the editors).

26. From Schmitt (1932, pp. 13, 14; *Der Begriff des Politischen*); see, however, for the legacies of dualist thinking already Hegel, *Grundlinien der Philosophie des Rechts*, Annex of §324.

27. See especially Kolnai (1933, p. 1); Strauss (1932, p. 728).

28. See on this point Croce (1914, p. 117).

29. See also Kolnai (1933, p. 6).

30. From Alexander Pope's translation of the *Iliad* (1899) (the translator).
31. Von Clausewitz (1918, pp. 640–1); see also Palat (1921, p. 350).

4   On the Concept of Political Disputes

1. The aspect of asserting power (which is also called the 'politics of prestige'), is not of relevance here.
2. The comments of Kunz (1931) are for our treatise without any theoretical
   value; see however Heller (1927) and especially Bourquin (1931); see also
   my articles "Die völkerrechtlichen Ergebnisse der Tagung der Deutschen
   Gesellschaft für Völkerrecht" (1929) and "Stresemann als Schöpfer der
   deutschen Völkerrechtspolitik" (1930).
3. Bourquin (1931).
4. We assume that Morgenthau had in mind to eventually elaborate and
   publish his yet unpublished manuscript on "*The Derivation of the Political
   from the Nature of Man*", written in German in 1930 as *Über die Herkunft des
   Politischen aus dem Wesen des Menschen*; see in the editors' Introduction
   and in the respective references (the editors).
5. See article 19 of the Covenant of the League of Nations.
6. This results in the fact that the essentially static nature of the international legal bodies does not constitute in itself an exceptional and
   isolated fact, but rather the obvious sign of the abnormal state of international law.
7. See Bourquin (1931).
8. See especially Smend (1923, 1928).
9. See Decencière-Ferrandière (1929, p. 431); Brierly (1928); Baumgarten
   (1931); Heller (1927, pp. 125, 126, 129); Husserl (1925, p. 95).
10. As of May 1933.
11. This is true in the Franco-Italian relationship where, for an identical rea-
    son, it was not even possible to initiate a discussion. See Strisower (1919,
    1922); Nippold (1907, 1908); Husserl (1925, pp. 84, 85, 91).
12. See, however, especially the observations of Ferrero (1928, pp. 105–18);
    Fenwick (1921); Borchard (1924, p.132); Balch (1925, p. 80); Schmitt (1926,
    p. 43) Wolzendorff (1919, pp. 41, 50); Weber (1922, p. 20); Giraud (1922,
    p. 486); Jerusalem (1920, p. 137); Bentham (1915, p. 87); Sinzheimer
    (1917, p. 32); Stuycken (1923, pp. 95, 100); Ratzenhofer (1893, pp. 132–3,
    141); Strisower (1922); Potter (1922, p. 257); Thieme (1927, p. 53); Hold-
    Ferneck (1932, p. 223); Bourquin (1931, p. 188); Brierly (1928).
13. Guggenheim (1931, p. 74); Guggenheim (1932, pp. 111, 121).
14. See on this point of view, Husserl (1925, p. 100); Kolnai (1933, p. 34).

5   Conclusion

1. Morgenthau refers here to his PhD thesis; see note 1 under "Preface" (the
   editors).

References

Balch, Thomas Willing (1925), *Rechtliche und politische Fragen zwischen Nationen*, Würzburg: Memmiger.

Barandon, Paul (1933), *Le système juridique de la Société des Nations pour la prévention de la guerre*, Geneva: Kundig.

Baumgarten, A. (1931), "Souveränität und Völkerrecht", *Zeitschrift für ausländisches öffentliches Recht und Völkerrecht*, Vol. 2, No. 1, pp. 305–34.

Bentham, Jeremy (1915), *Grundsätze für ein künftiges Völkerrecht und einen dauernden Frieden*, Halle: Niemeyer.

Borchard, Ediwn Montefiore (1924), "The Distinction between Legal and Political Questions", *ASIL Annual Meeting Proceedings*.

Brierly, James L. (1928), *TheLaw of Nations: An Introduction to the Introduction Law of Peace*, Oxford: Clarendon.

Büchi, Robert (1914), *Geschichte der panamerikanischen Bewegung*, Breslau: J. U. Kern.

Burckhardt, Walther (1927), *Die Organisation der Rechtsgemeinschaft*, Basel: Helbing & Lichterhahn.

Bourquin, Maurice (1931), "Règles général du droit de la paix", *Recueil des Cours* (1931 – I), No. 35, pp. 1–232, http://gallica.bnf.fr/ark:/12148/bpt6k6130851b/f11.planchecontact.r=recueil%20de%20cours.langEN

Castberg, Frede (1925), "La compétence des tribunaux internationaux", *Revue de Droit international et de législation comparée*, No. 3, pp. 310–38.

Decencière-Ferrandière, André (1929), "Quelques réflexions touchant le règlement des conflits internationaux", *Revue générale de Droit international public*, No. 36, pp. 416–51.

Dimitch, Velimir N. (1930), *La courtoisie internationale*, Paris: Recueil Sirey.

Fauchille, Paul (1921), *Traité de droit international public*, t.III, Paris: Rousseau.

Fenwick, Charles G. (1921), "Law: The Prerequisite of an International Court", *Annals of American Academy of Political and Social Science*, No. 96, pp. 118–23.

Ferrero, Guglielmo (1928), *Die Einheit der Welt*, Berlin: Fischer.

Gallus (1930), "L'acte générale d'arbitrage", *Revue de Droit international et de législation comparative*, No. 11, pp. 190–246.

Giraud, Emile (1922), "De la valeur et des rapports des notions de droit de politique dans l'ordre national", *La Revue générale de droit international public*, No. 29, pp. 473–514.

Guggenheim, Paul (1931), *Les Mesures provisoires de procédure internationale et leur influence sur le développement du droit des gens*, Paris: Recueil Sirey.

Guggenheim, Paul (1932), *Der Völkerbund*, Leipzig: B. G. Teubner.

Hegel, G. W. F. (1911), *Grundlinien der Philosophie des Rechts*, Leipzig: Felix Meiner.

Heller, Hermann (1927), *Die Souveränität: ein Beitrag zur Theorie des Staats- und Völkerrechts*, Berlin: de Gruyter.

Hoijer, Olof (1926), *Le Pacte de la Société des Nations*, Paris: Éditions Spés.

Hold-Ferneck, Alexander (1932), *Lehrbuch des Völkerrechts*, vol. II, Leipzig: Meiner.

Homer (1996), *The Iliad*, trans. Alexander Pope, London: Penguin.

Hostie, Jean (1928), "Différends justiciables et non justiciables", *Revue de Droit international et de législation comparée*, Vol. 9, No. 3, pp. 263–81.

Huber, Max (1908), "Die Fortbildung des Völkerrecht auf dem Gebiete des Prozeß- und Landkriegsrechts durch die II. Internationale Friedenskonferenz in Haag 1907", *Jahrbuch des öffentlichen Rechts*, No. 2, pp. 470–611.

Husserl, Gerhart (1925), *Rechtskraft und Rechtsgeltung*, Berlin: Springer.

Jerusalem, Franz Wilhelm (1920), *Soziologie des Rechts*, Jena: Fischer.

Kaufmann, Erich (1932), *Probleme der internationalen Gerichtsbarkeit*, Leipzig: B. G. Teubner.

Kolnai, Aurel (1933), "Der Inhalt der Politik", *Zeitschrift für die gesamte Staatswissenschaft*, Vol. 94, No. 1, pp. 1–38.

Kroner, Richard (1931), *Kulturphilosophische Grundlegung der Politik*, Berlin: Junker und Dünnhaupt.

Kunz, Josef Laurenz (1931), "Statisches und dynamisches Völkerrecht", in Alfred Verdross and Josef Dobretsberger (eds), *Gesellschaft, Recht und Staat, herausg. von Verdross*, Vienna: Sauer & Auvermann.

Lammasch, Heinrich (1912), "Über isolierte und institutionelle Schieds-gerichte", *Jahrbuch des öffentlichen Rechts*, No. 6.

Lauterpacht, Hersch (1930), "La théorie des différends non justiciables en droit international", *Recueil des Cours*, Vol. 34, No. 4, pp. 493–654.

Le Fur, Louis (1931), *Précis de droit international public*, Paris: Dalloz.

Mariotte, Pierre (1926), *Les limites actuelles de la compétence de la Société des Nations*, Paris: Pedone.

Marshall-Brown, M.M. and Politis, Nicolas (1922), "Classification des conflits justiciables", *Annuaire de l'Institut de Droit international*, http://www.idi-iil.org/idiF/resolutionsF/1922_greno_01_fr.pdf

Meinecke, Friedrich (1925), *Die Idee der Staatsraison in der neueren Geschichte*, Munich: R. Oldenbourg.

Morgenthau, Hans J. (1929), "Die völkerrechtlichen Ergebnisse der Tagung der deutschen Gesellschaft für Völkerrecht", *Die Justiz*, Vol. 4, No. 6, pp. 621–24.

Morgenthau, Hans J. (1930), "Stresemann als Schöpfer der deutschen Völkerrechtspolitik", *Die Justiz*, Vol. 5, No. 3, pp. 169–76.

Nelson, Leonard (1924) *System der philosophischen Rechtslehre und Politik*, Leipzig: Veit & Comp.

Nippold, Otfried (1907), *Die Fortbildung des Verfahrens in völkerrechtlichen Streitigkeiten*, Leipzig: Duncker & Humblot.

Nippold, Otfried (1908), *Die zweite Haager Friedenskonferenz*, Leipzig: Duncker & Humblot.

Palat, General (1921), *La philosophie de la guerre d'après Clausewitz*, Paris: Lavauzelle.

Phillimore, Lord (1921), "Signature de la clause facultative de la Cour permanente de Justice internationale", *Annuaire de Droit International de l'Institut*, No. 28, pp. 201, 202.

Plessner, Helmuth (1931), *Macht und menschliche Natur*, Berlin: Junker und Dünnhaupt.

Politis, Nicolas (1924), *La justice internationale*, Paris: Hachette.

Potter, Pitman B. (1922), *An Introduction to the Study of International Organisation*, New York: Appleton-Century-Crofts.

Ratzenhofer, Gustav (1893), *Wesen und Zweck der Politik: als Theil der Sociologie und Grundlage der Staatswissenschaften*, Leipzig: Brockhaus.

Ray, Jean (1930), *Commentaire du Pacte de la Société des Nations*, Paris: Recueil Sirey.

Redslob, Robert (1927), *Théorie de la Société des Nations*, Paris: Rousseau.

Rousseau, Charles (1927), *La compétence de la Société des Nations dans le règlement des conflits internationaux*, Paris: Imprimerie administrative centrale.

Scelle, Georges (1919), *Le Pacte des Nations et sa liaison avec le Traité de Paix*, Paris: Recueil Sirey.

Scelle, Georges (1932), *Précis de droit des gens*, Paris: Recueil Sirey.

Schindler, Dietrich (1927), "Werdende Rechte", in Giacometti Zaccaria and Dietrich Schindler (eds), *Festgabe für Fritz Fleiner zum 60. Geburtstag*, Tübingen: Mohr, pp. 400–31.

Schmitt, Carl (1926), *Die Kernfrage des Völkerbundes*, Berlin: Dümmler.

Schmitt, Carl (1927), "Der Begriff des Politischen", *Archiv für Sozialwissenschaft und Sozialpolitik*, No. 58, pp. 1–33.

Schmitt, Carl (1930), *Hugo Preuss, sein Staatsbegriff und seine Stellung in der deutschen Staatslehre*, Tübingen: Mohr.

Schmitt, Carl (1930), *Staatsethik und pluralistischer Staat*, Berlin: Duncker & Humblot.

Schmitt, Carl (1931), *Der Hüter der Verfassung*, Tübingen: Mohr.

Schmitt, Carl (1932), *Der Begriff des Politischen*, Berlin: Duncker & Humblot.

Schücking, Walther (1918), *Die völkerrechtliche Lehre des Weltkriegs*, Leipzig: Veit & Comp.

Schücking, Walther and Hans Wehberg (1924), *Die Satzung des Völkerbunds*, Berlin: Vahlen.

Schumpeter, Joseph (1919), "Zur Soziologie der Imperialismen", *Archiv für Sozialwissenschaft und Sozialpolitik*, No. 54, pp. 1–39.

Sinzheimer, Hugo (1917), *Völkerrechtsgeist: Rede zur Einführung in das Programm der Zentralstelle "Völkerrecht", gehalten auf der Gründungsversammlung am 3. Dezember 1916*, Leipzig: Verlag Naturwissenschaften.

Smend, Rudolf (1923), *Die politische Gewalt im Verfassungsstaat und das Problem der Staatsform*, in *Festgabe der Berliner juristischen Fakultät für Wilhelm Kahl*, Tübingen: Mohr, pp. 3–25.

Smend, Rudolf (1928), *Verfassung und Verfassungsrecht*, Munich: Duncker & Humblot.

Stammler, Rudolf (1911), *Theorie der Rechtswissenschaft*, Halle: Buchhandlung des Waisenhauses.

Strauss, Leo (1932), "Anmerkungen zu Carl Schmitt, Der Begriff des Politischen", *Archiv für Sozialwissenschaft und Sozialpolitik*, No. 67, pp. 732–49.

Strisower, Leo (1919), *Der Krieg und die Völkerrechtsordnung*, Vienna: Manz.

Strisower, Leo (1922), "Les doubles impositions", *Annuaire de Droit International de l'Institut*, http://www.idi-iil.org/idiF/resolutionsF/1922_greno_02_fr.pdf.

Strupp, Karl (1914), *Internationale Schiedsgerichtsbarkeit*, Berlin: Rothschild.

Strupp, Karl (1918), *Gegenwartsfragen des Völkerrechts*, Gotha: Perthes.

Strupp, Karl (1929), *Schiedsgerichts-, Gerichts- und Vergleichsverträge des deutschen Reichs*, Berlin: Stilke.

Strupp, Karl (1932), *Grundzüge des positiven Völkerrechts*, Bonn: Röhrscheid.

Stuycken, A. A. H. (1923), *La Société des Nations et l'intégrité territoriale*, Leiden: Brill.

Thieme, Hans Wilhelm (1927), *Die Fortbildung der internationalen Schiedsgerichtsbarkeit seit dem Weltkrieg*, Leipzig: Noske.

Triepel, Heinrich (1923), Streitigkeiten zwischen Reich und Ländern, in *Festgabe der Berliner juristischen Fakultät für Wilhelm Kahl*, Tübingen: Mohr, pp. 51–118.

Vattel, Emmerich de (1758), *Le droit des gens*, Leiden.

Verdross, Alfred (1926), *Die Verfassung der Völkerrechtsgemeinschaft*, Vienna: Springer.

Verzijl, J. H. W. (1925), "La classification des différends internationaux et la nature du litige anglo-turc relatif au vilayet du Mossoul", *Revue de Droit International*, Vol. 6, No. 6, pp. 732–59.

von Clausewitz, Karl (1918), *Vom Kriege*, Berlin-Leipzig: Behr.

von Hippel, Fritz (1930), *Zur Gesetzmäßigkeit juristischer Systembildung*, Berlin: Junker und Dünnhaupt.

Weber, Max (1922), *Grundriss der Socialökonomik, 3. Abt. Wirtschaft und Gesellschaft*, Tübingen: Mohr.

Wehberg, Hans (1911), *Kommentar zu dem Haager Abkommen betreffend die friedliche Erledigung internationalen Streitigkeiten vom 18.10.1907*, Tübingen: Mohr.

Wehberg, Hans (1912), *Das Problem eines internationalen Staatengerichtshofes*, Munich: Duncker & Humblot.

Wolzendorff, Kurt (1919), *Die Lüge des Völkerrechts*, Leipzig: Der neue Geist.

Annex 1

Bibliography of Hans J. Morgenthau (Published and Unpublished Academic Work in Chronological Order)

(1929a), *Die internationale Rechtspflege, ihr Wesen und ihre Grenzen*, Leipzig: Universitätsverlag von Robert Noske.

(1929b), "Die völkerrechtlichen Ergebnisse der Tagung der deutschen Gesellschaft für Völkerrecht", *Die Justiz*, Vol. 4, No. 6, pp. 621–4.

(1930a), "Stresemann als Schöpfer der deutschen Völkerrechtspolitik", *Die Justiz*, Vol. 5, No. 3, pp. 169–76.

(1930b), "Der Selbstmord mit gutem Gewissen. Zur Kritik des Pazifismus und der neuen deutschen Kriegsphilosophie" (unpublished manuscript, Manuscript Division, Library of Congress, Washington DC, Box 96).

(1930c), "Über die Herkunft des Politischen aus dem Wesen des Menschen" (unpublished manuscript, Manuscript Division, Library of Congress, Washington DC, Box 151).

(1932), "Der Kampf der deutschen Staatslehre um die Wirklichkeit des Staates" (unpublished manuscript, Manuscript Division, Library of Congress, Washington DC, Box 110).

(1933), *La notion du "politique" et la théorie des différends internationaux*, Paris: Recueil Sirey.

(1934a), *La Réalité des normes. En particulier des normes du droit international. Fondement d'une théorie des normes*, Paris: Félix Alcan.

(1934b), "Über den Sinn der Wissenschaft in dieser Zeit und über die Bestimmung des Menschen" (unpublished manuscript, Manuscript Division, Library of Congress, Washington DC, Box 151).

(1934–1935), "Einige logische Bemerkungen zu Carl Schmitt's Begriff des Politischen" (unpublished manuscript, Manuscript Division, Library of Congress, Washington DC, Box 151).

(1935a), "Théorie des sanctions internationales", *Revue de Droit International de législation comparée*, No. 3–4, pp. 474–503 and 809–36.

(1935b), "Derecho internacional publico. Introducción y conceptos fundamentales" (unpublished manuscript, Manuscript Division, Library of Congress, Washington DC, Box 190).

(1936), "Positivisme mal compris et théorie réaliste du Droit international", in Silvio A. Zavala (ed.), *Colección de estudios históricos, jurídicos, pedagógicos y literarios. Homenaje a D. Rafael Altamira*, Madrid: C. Bermejo, pp. 446–65.

(1937), "Kann in unserer Zeit eine objektive Moralordnung aufgestellt werden? Wenn ja, worauf kann sie gegründet werden? Kennwort: Metaphysik" (unpublished manuscript, Manuscript Division, Library of Congress, Washington DC, Box 112).

(1938), "The End of Switzerland's 'Differential' Neutrality", *American Journal of International Law*, Vol. 32, No. 3, pp. 558–62.

(1939), "The Resurrection of Neutrality in Europe", *American Political Science Review*, Vol. 23, No. 3, pp. 473–86.

(1940), "Positivism, Functionalism, and International Law", *American Journal of International Law*, Vol. 34, pp. 260–84.

(1943), "Implied Regulatory Powers in Administrative Law", *Iowa Law Review*, Vol. 23, No. 4, pp. 576–612.

(1944), "The Limitations of Science and the Problem of Social Planning", *Ethics*, Vol. 54, No. 3, pp. 174–85.

(1945a), "The Machiavellian Utopia", *Ethics*, Vol. 55, No. 2, pp. 145–7.

(1945b), "The Scientific Solution of Social Conflicts", *Approaches to National Unity*, New York: Conference on Science, Philosophy and Religion in their Relation to the Democratic Way of Life, pp. 419–43.

(1945c), "The Evil of Politics and the Ethics of Evil", *Ethics*, Vol. 56, No. 1, pp. 1–18.

(1945–46) "Diplomacy", *Yale Law Journal*, No. 55, pp. 1067–80.

(1946a), "Nazism", in Joseph S. Boncek (ed.), *Twentieth Century Political Thought*, New York: Philosophical Library, pp. 132–48.

(1946b), (ed.), *Peace, Security and the United Nations*, Chicago: University of Chicago Press.

(1947a), *Scientific Man vs Power Politics*, London: Latimer House.

(1947b), "Ethics and Politics", in Lyman Bryson, Louis Finkelstein and R. M. MacIver (eds), *Approaches to Group Understanding*, New York: Harper & Brothers, pp. 319–20.

(1948a), "The Twilight of International Morality", *Ethics*, Vol. 58, No. 2, pp. 9–99.

(1948b), "The Political Science of E. H. Carr", *World Politics*, Vol. 1, No. 1, pp. 127–34.

(1948c), "World Politics in the Mid-twentieth Century", *Review of Politics*, Vol. 10, No. 2, pp. 154–73.

(1948d), "The Problem of Sovereignty Reconsidered", *Columbia Law Review*, Vol. 48, No. 3, pp. 341–65.

(1948e), *Politics Among Nations: The Struggle for Power and Peace*, New York: A. A. Knopf (1st edition; also 1954, 1960, 1967, 1972, 1978, 1985, 1993, 2006).

(1949a), "Conduct of American Foreign Policy", *Parliamentary Affairs*, Vol. 3, No. 1, pp. 2–16.

(1949b), "The Limits of Practicability in the Social Sciences. Section IV.B of the Steering Committee on the Social Science and Values Project Report"

148 *Annex 1*

(unpublished manuscript, Manuscript Division, Library of Congress, Washington DC, Box 74).

(1949c), "National Interest and Moral Principles in Foreign Policy: The Primacy of National Interest", *American Scholar*, No. 18.

(1950a), "The Mainsprings of American Foreign Policy: The National Interest vs Moral Abstractions", *American Political Science Review*, Vol. 44, No. 4, pp. 833–54.

(1950b), "The Decline of Liberty and Mr Laski", *Common Cause*, Vol. 3, No. 8, pp. 440–4.

(1950c), "The Conquest of the United States by Germany", *Bulletin of the Atomic Scientists*, Vol. 6, No. 1, pp. 21–6.

(1950d), "The H-bomb and After", *Bulletin of the Atomic Scientists*, Vol. 6, No. 3, pp. 76–9.

(1950e), "The Evil of Power. A Critical Study of de Jouvenel's On Power", *Review of Metaphysics*, Vol. 3, No. 4, pp. 507–17.

(1951a), *In Defense of the National Interest: A Critical Examination of American Foreign Policy*, New York: Alfred A. Knopf.

(1951b), "The Policy of the USA", *Political Quarterly*, Vol. 22, No. 1, pp. 43–56.

(1951c), "The Moral Dilemma in Foreign Policy", *Yearbook of World Affairs*, No. 5, pp. 12–36.

(1951d), "The Unfinished Business of US Foreign Policy", *Wisconsin Idea*, Vol. 4, No. 1, pp. 2–3, 19 and 30–31.

(1951e), (ed.), *Germany and the Future of Europe*, Chicago: University of Chicago Press.

(1952a), "What is the National Interest of the United States?", *Annals of the American Academy of Political and Social Science*, No. 282, pp. 1–7.

(1952b), "Les area studies et l'étude des relations nternationales", *UNESCO Bulletin international des sciences sociales*, Vol. 4, No. 4, pp. 685–94.

(1952c), "Building a European Federation: The Schuman Plan and European Federation", *Proceedings of the American Society of International Law*, No. 46, pp. 130–4.

(1954a), "The Yardstick of National Interest", *Annals of the American Academy of Political and Social Science*, No. 296, pp. 77–84.

(1954b), "The New United Nations and the Revision of the Charter", *Review of Politics*, Vol. 16, No. 1, pp. 3–21.

(1954c), "The Political and Military Strategy of the United States", *Bulletin of the Atomic Scientists*, Vol. 10, No. 8, pp. 323–7.

(1955a), "Foreign Policy: The Conservative School", *World Politics*, Vol. 7, No. 2, pp. 284–92.

(1955b), "United States Policy toward Africa", in Calvin Stillman (ed.), *Africa in the Modern World*, Chicago: University of Chicago Press, pp. 317–25.

(1955c), "Government Administration and Security", *Current History*, Vol. 29, No. 170, pp. 210–16.

(1955d), "La strategia politica e militare degli stati uniti", *Il Politico*, Vol. 20, No. 2, pp. 232–42.

(1955e), "Reflections on the State of Political Science", *Review of Politics*, Vol. 17, No. 4, pp. 431–60.

(1956a), "The 1954 Geneva Conference: An Assessment", in American Friends of Vietnam (ed.), *America's Stake in Vietnam*, New York: American Friends of Vietnam, pp. 64–70.

(1956b), "The Art of Diplomatic Negotiation", in Leonard D. White (ed.), *The State of the Social Sciences*, Chicago: University of Chicago Press, pp. 404–14.

(1956c), "Is Atomic War Really Impossible", *Bulletin of the Atomic Scientists*, Vol. 12, No. 1, pp. 7–9.

(1957a), "Neutrality and Neutralism", *Yearbook of World Affairs*, No. 2, pp. 47–75.

(1957b), "The Paradoxes of Nationalism", *Yale Review*, Vol. 46, No. 4, pp. 481–96.

(1957c), "Der Pazifismus des Atomzeitalters", *Der Monat*, Vol. 10, No. 109, pp. 3–8.

(1957d), "The Revolution in US Foreign Policy", *Commentary*, Vol. 23, No. 2, pp. 101–5.

(1957e), "Sources of Tension between Western Europe and the United States", *Annals of the American Academy of Political and Social Science*, No. 312, pp. 22–8.

(1957f), "The Dilemmas of Freedom", *American Political Science Review*, Vol. 51, No. 3, pp. 714–23.

(1957g), "Les dangers du 'néo-pazifisme'", *Preuves*, No. 80, pp. 66–70.

(1957h), "RIAS Funk-Universität. Wirkungsformen traditioneller und demokratisch legitimierter Diplomatie" (broadcast: November 6), (unpublished manuscript, Manuscript Division, Library of Congress, Washington DC, Box 199).

(1958a), *The Dilemmas of Politics*, Chicago: University of Chicago Press.

(1958b), "Realism in International Politics", *Naval War College Review*, Vol. 10, No. 5, pp. 1–15.

(1958c), "Alliances", *Confluence*, Vol. 6, No. 4, pp. 311–34.

(1958d), "The Crisis of the Atlantic Alliance", *Western World*, No. 12, pp. 13–16.

(1958e), "Should we Negotiate Now?", *Commentary*, Vol. 25, No. 3, pp. 192–9.

(1958f), "The United Nations", *Commentary*, Vol. 25, No. 10, pp. 375–82.

(1959a), "Dilemmas of Politics", *International Affairs*, Vol. 35, No. 4, p. 502.

(1959b), "The Nature and Limits of a Theory of International Relations", in William T. R. Fox (ed.), *Theoretical Aspects of International Relations*, Notre Dame: University of Notre Dame Press, pp. 15–28.

(1959c), "Education and World Politics", *Daedalus*, Vol. 88, No. 1, pp. 121–38.

(1959d), "Soviet Policy and World Conquest", *Current History*, Vol. 37, No. 219, pp. 290–4.

(1959e), "Contradictions in US China Policy", in Urban Whitaker (ed.), *Foundations of US China Policy*, Berkeley: Pacifica Foundation, pp. 98–105.

(1959f), "The Decline of Democratic Government", *University of Chicago Magazine*, No. 1, pp. 5–8.

(1960a), *The Purpose of American Politics*, New York: Alfred A. Knopf.

(1960b), "The Intellectual and Moral Dilemma of History", *Christianity and Crisis*, Vol. 20, No. 1, pp. 3–6.

(1960c), "The Problem of German Reunification", *Annals of the American Academy of Political and Social Science*, No. 330, pp. 124–32.

(1960d), "Reflexiones sobre la politica exterior de la union sovietica", *Revista de ciencias socials de la Universidad de Puerto Rico*, pp. 437–45.

(1960e), "The Social Crisis in America: Hedonism of Status Quo", *Chicago Review*, Vol. 14, No. 2, pp. 69–88.

(1960f), "The Demands of Prudence", *Worldview*, Vol. 3, No. 6, pp. 6–7.

(1960g), *The Crisis of American Foreign Policy: The Brian McMahon Lectures*, Mansfield: University of Connecticut.

(1961a), *The Leo Baeck Memorial Lecture 4: The Tragedy of German Jewish Liberalism*, New York: Leo Baeck Institute.

(1961b), "The Containment Policy and the Rationale of the Alliance System", in Stephen Kertesz (ed.), *Theoretical Aspects of International Relations*, Notre Dame: University of Notre Dame Press, pp. 63–82.

(1961c), "Hauptprobleme der amerikanischen Außenpolitik", *Österreichische Zeitschrift für Außenpolitik*, Vol. 5, No. 1, pp. 302–15.

(1961d), "The Purpose of American Politics", *The Executive*, Vol. 5, No. 2, pp. 9–11.

(1961e), "The American Tradition in Foreign Policy", Roy C. Macridis (ed.), *Foreign Policy in World Politics*, Eaglewood Cliffs: Prentice-Hall, pp. 201–24.

(1961f), *Das Interesse der Atlantischen Gemeinschaft: Der Status Quo in Deutschland?* (unpublished manuscript, Archive for Christian-Democratic Policy, Konrad-Adenauer-Stiftung, shelfmark: 01-156-022/2).

(1962a), *Politics in the Twentieth Century, Vol. I, The Decline of Democratic Politics*, Chicago: University of Chicago Press.

(1962b), *Politics in the Twentieth Century, Vol. II, The Impasse of American Foreign Policy*, Chicago: University of Chicago Press.

(1962c), *Politics in the Twentieth Century, Vol. III, The Restoration of American Politics*, Chicago: University of Chicago Press.

(1962d), "Decision-making in the Nuclear Age", *Bulletin of the Atomic Scientists*, Vol. 18, No. 10, pp. 7–8.

(1962e), "L'Etat universel et les institutions supranationales", *Comprendre*, No. 23–4, pp. 1–11.

(1962f), "The Roots of America's China Policy", *China Quarterly* (April–June), pp. 45–50.

(1962g), "The Real Issue Between the United States and the Quest for Wholeness", in Jerold N. Willmore (ed.), *Critical Issues and Decisions*, Washington DC: United States Department of Agriculture Graduate School, pp. 69–80.

(1962h), "Love and Power", *Commentary*, March, published by the American Jewish Committee, pp. 247–51.

(1963a), *Macht und Frieden: Grundlegung einer Theorie der internationalen Politik*, Gütersloh: C. Bertelsmann Verlag.

(1963b), "Preface to a Political Theory of Foreign Aid", in Robert C. Goldwin (ed.), *Why Foreign Aid?*, Chicago: Rand McNally, pp. 70–89.

(1963c), "The American Political Legacy", in William H. Nelson (ed.), *Theory and Practice in American Politics*, Houston: Rice University, pp. 139–49.

(1963d), "The Impartiality of the International Peace", in Salo Engel and Rudolf A. Métall (eds), *Law, State, and International Legal Order: Essays in Honour of Hans Kelsen*, Knoxville: University of Tennessee Press, pp. 209–23.

(1963e), "The Political Conditions for an International Police Force", *International Organization*, Vol. 17, No. 2, pp. 393–403.

(1963f), "A World State?", *Pax Romana Journal*, No. 1, pp. 7–11.

(1964a), "The Nature and Use of Power and its Influence upon State Goals and Strategies", *Naval War College Review*, Vol. 16, No. 6, pp. 18–30.

(1964b), "Death in the Nuclear Age", *Context*, Vol. 2, No. 1, pp. 25–7.

(1964c), "The Four Paradoxes of Nuclear Strategy", *American Political Science Review*, Vol. 58, No. 1, pp. 22–35.

(1964d), "Modern Science and Political Power", *Columbia Law Review*, Vol. 64, No. 4, pp. 1386–409.

(1964e), *The Crisis of the Western Alliance: Advance Study Paper No. 7*, Washington DC: Georgetown University, Center for Strategic Studies.

(1964f), "Krise im westlichen Bündnis", *Wehrkunde*, No. 13, pp. 628–33.

(1964g), "Politica exterior y estregia military en la edad nuclear", *Revista de a Facultad de Derecho de México*, Vol. 14, No. 54, pp. 367–88.

(1964h), (ed.), *The Crossroad Papers: A Look into the Future*, New York: Norton.

(1965a), *Vietnam and the United States*, Washington DC: Public Affairs Press.

(1965b), *The Crisis of Communism: Paper No. 4*, Cincinnati: University of Cincinnati, Center for the Study of US Foreign Policy of the Department of Political Science.

(1965c), "Law, Politics and the United Nations", *Commercial Law Journal*, Vol. 70, No. 5, pp. 121–4 and 135.

(1965d), "The Writer's Duty and his Predicament", *Hudson Review*, Vol. 28, No. 2, pp. 269–74.

(1965e), "The Vietnam Crisis and China", *Bulletin of the Atomic Scientists*, Vol. 21, No. 6, p. 27.

(1966a), "Introduction", in David Mitrany (ed.), *A Working Peace System*, Chicago: Quadrangle, pp. 7–11.

(1966b), "American Foreign Policy in Asia", *Barat Faculty Review*, Vol. 1, No. 1, pp. 3–9.

(1967a), "Common Sense and Theories of International Relations", *International Affairs*, No. 21, pp. 207–14.

(1967b), "Grundfragen einer neuen Außenpolitik für die Vereinigten Staaten", *Europa-Archiv*, No. 19, pp. 689–96.

(1967c), "A New Foreign Policy for the United States: Basic Issues", *Bulletin of the Atomic Scientists*, Vol. 23, No. 1, pp. 7–11.

(1967d), "To Intervene or not to Intervene", *Foreign Affairs*, Vol. 45, No. 3, pp. 92–103.

(1967e), "Die Regierung Johnson und die Intellektuellen", *Atomzeitalter*, No. 1–2, pp. 18–26.

(1968a), "Organization of a Power System: Unilateralism and the Balance of the Power", *Naval War College Review*, Vol. 20, No. 7, pp. 3–11.

(1968b), "The United States and China", *International Studies*, Vol. 10, No. 1–2, pp. 23–34.

(1968c), "US Misadventure in Vietnam", *Indian & Foreign Review*, Vol. 5, No. 13, pp. 18–19.

(1968d), "US Misadventure in Vietnam", *Current History*, No. 45, pp. 29–34.

(1968e), "Krieg als Paradoxon", *Neues Forum*, No. 179–80, pp. 708–10.

(1968f), "The United States and China", in Tang Tsou (ed.), *China's Policies in Asia and America's Alternatives*, Chicago: University of Chicago Press, pp. 93–105.

(1968g), "But are they Allowed to do That?", *Christian Science Monitor*, July 19, p. 9.

(1969a), *A New Foreign Policy for the United States*, New York: Praeger.

(1969b), "The United States and China: A Study in Real Issues", *Political Science Review*, Vol. 8, No. 1, pp. 1–11.

(1969c), "The United States as a World Power: A Balance-sheet", *International Studies*, Vol. 11, No. 2, pp. 111–48.

(1970a), *Truth and Power: Essays of a decade, 1960–1970*, London: Pall Mall Press.

(1970b), "Der Friede im nuklearen Zeitalter", in Oskar Schatz (ed.), *Der Friede im nuklearen Zeitalter. Eine Kontroverse zwischen Realisten und Utopisten. 4. Salzburger Humanismusgespräch*, Munich: Manz Verlag, pp. 34–62.

(1970c), "International Relations: Quantitative and Qualitative Approaches", in Norman D. Palmer (ed.), *A Design for International Relations Research: Scope, Theory, Methods, and Relevance*, Philadelphia: American Academy of Political and Social Science, pp. 67–71.

(1971a), "Thought and Action in Politics", *Social Research*, Vol. 38, No. 4, pp. 611–32.

(1971b), "Power as a Political Concept", in Roland Young (ed.), *Approaches to the Study of Politics*, Evanston: Northwestern University Press, pp. 66–77.

(1971c), "Changes and Chances in American–Soviet Relations", *Foreign Affairs*, Vol. 49, No. 3, pp. 429–41.

(1972a), *Science: Servant or Master?*, New York: New American Library.

(1972b), "The American Crisis", in James Dorothy Buckton (ed.), *Outside, Looking In: Critiques of American Policies and Institutions, Left and Right*, New York: Harper and Row, pp. 350–73.

(1972c), "Das internationale System an der Wende?", *Schweizer Monatshefte*, Vol. 52, No. 8, pp. 556–61.

(1972d), "Soviet Perspectives and Dynamics: The Soviet Union, China and Japan", in Norton T. Dodge (ed.), *The Soviets in Asia*, Mechanicsville: Cremona Foundation, pp. 41–4.

(1972e), "Der neue Feudalismus. Ein Paradoxon vereitelter Regierung", in Oskar Schatz (ed.), *Auf dem Weg zur hörigen Gesellschaft?*, Graz: Styria, pp. 119–35.

(1973a), "The Ideological and Political Dynamics of the Middle Eastern Policy of the Soviet Union", in M. Confino and S. Shamir (eds), *The USSR and the Middle East*, Jerusalem: Israel Universities Press, pp. 71–6.

(1973b), "Justice and Power", *Social Research*, Vol. 40, No. 3, pp. 163–75.

(1973c), "Macht und Ohnmacht des Menschen im technologischen Zeitalter", in Oskar Schatz (ed.), *Was wird aus dem Menschen? Der Fortschritt – Analysen und Warnungen bedeutender Denker*, Graz: Verlag Styria, pp. 47–60.

(1974a), "The Permanent Values in the Old Diplomacy", in Stephen D. Kertesz and M.A. Fitzsimons (eds), *Diplomacy in a Changing World*, Westport: Greenwood Press, pp. 11–20.

(1974b), "The United States and Europe in a Decade of Detente", in Wolfram Hanrieder (ed.), *The United States and Western Europe*, Cambridge: Winthrop.

(1974c), "Decline of Democratic Government", *The New Republic*, November 9, pp. 13–18.

(1975), "The Decline of the West", *Partisan Review*, Vol. 42, No. 4, pp. 508–16.

(1976a), "Hannah Arendt 1906–1975", *Political Theory*, Vol. 4, No. 1, pp. 5–8.

(1976b), "Reality and Illusion", *Middle East Review*, No. 8, pp. 5–9.

(1976c), "The Founding Fathers and Foreign Policy: Implications for the Late 20th Century", *Orbis*, Vol. 20, No. 1, pp. 15–25.

(1977a), "Hannah Arendt on Totalitarianism and Democracy", *Social Research*, Vol. 44, No. 1, pp. 127–31.

(1977b), "The Pathology of American Power", *International Security*, Vol. 1, No. 3, pp. 3–20.

(1979), *Human Rights and Foreign Policy*, New York: Council on Religion and International Affairs.

(1980), "Developments in Foreign Policy", in CTV Corporation (ed.), *American Foreign Policy in the '80s*, Dallas: CTV Corporation, pp. 40–4.

(1984), "Fragment of an Intellectual Autobiography: 1904–1932", in Kenneth W. Thompson (ed.), *Truth and Tragedy: A Tribute to Hans J. Morgenthau*, Piscataway: Transaction, pp. 1–17.

(1985), *Politics Among Nations: The Struggle for Power and Peace*, New York: Alfred A. Knopf.

(2004), *Political Theory and International Affairs: Hans J. Morgenthau on Aristotle's The Politics*, ed. Anthony F. Lang Jr, Westport: Praeger.

together with Kenneth W. Thompson (1950), *Principles and Problems of International Politics*, New York: Alfred A. Knopf.

together with James P. Warburg (1960), "The Problem of German Reunification", *Annals of the American Academy of Political and Social Science*, No. 330, pp. 124–32.

together with Kenneth W. Thompson and Jerald C. Brauer (1968), *US Policy in the Far East: Ideology, Religion, and Superstition*, New York: Council on Religion and International Affairs.

together with Marshall D. Shulman (1974), "Approaches to Detente", *Congress Bi-weekly*, Vol. 41, No. 5, pp. 5–9.

together with Ethel Person (1978), "The Roots of Narcissism", *Partisan Review*, Vol. 45, No. 3, pp. 337–47.

(1984), "Postscript to the Transaction edition: Bernard Johnson's interview with Hans J. Morgenthau", in Kenneth W. Thompson (ed.), *Truth and Tragedy. A Tribute to Hans J. Morgenthau*, Piscataway, NJ: Transaction, pp. 333–86.

Annex 2

Biography of Hans J. Morgenthau, Including the Publication Years of His Major Monographs

1904: Birth in Cobourg, Germany

Hans Joachim Morgenthau was born into a Jewish middle-class family in Cobourg on February 17, 1904. Cobourg was then the capital of the duchy Saxe-Coburg-Gotha and is now situated on the northeastern edge of Bavaria. His father, Ludwig, was a physician and his mother Frieda, née Bachmann, the daughter of a wealthy merchant from nearby Bamberg. His parents were typical representatives of the liberal German Jews at that time who put considerable effort into becoming "proper Germans". Morgenthau received his middle name Joachim in honor of the sixth son of the Emperor Wilhelm II. Despite their efforts, the Morgenthaus were socially ostracized in a particularly anti-Semitic environment. In 1929, Cobourg became the first town in Germany where the Nazi Party (*Nationalsozialistische Deutsche Arbeiterpartei*, or NSDAP) was able to win an absolute majority in city council elections. Their son in particular suffered in his childhood and youth from this alienation. Morgenthau was the best student in the Lower Primary of the local grammar school, the *Casimirianum*, and as a result he was granted the right to give a farewell address to the graduates and to crown the statue of the school's founder, the Duke Johann Casimir. During his speech, local officials and citizens turned away and held their noses because of the "stinking Jew".

1923–27: Student of philosophy and law in Frankfurt, Munich, and Berlin

Morgenthau briefly studied philosophy in Frankfurt, before studying law in Munich and Berlin. The decision to study law was enforced by his father, but he could not prevent his son from continuing to pursue his humanistic interests. Morgenthau also studied history with Hermann Oncken and art history with Heinrich Wölfflin. During his law studies he also came into contact with the works of the most important figures of legal and social studies in Germany at that time: Max Weber, Hans Kelsen, Georg Jellinek, Georg Simmel, Jacob Burckhardt, and Carl Schmitt. Morgenthau was already acquainted with the work of Friedrich Nietzsche as he had read him extensively in his youth. Alienation still dominated his life, as evidenced in his membership of the fraternity *Thuringia*. Like the step taken to join the Scouts during his childhood, Morgenthau hoped to become socially accepted by joining the *Thuringia*.

1928–30: Doctorate and clerkship in Hugo Sinzheimer's law office in Frankfurt

After beginning his doctorate in Munich, Morgenthau soon relocated to the Prussian Frankfurt and finished his thesis *Die international Rechtspflege, ihr Wesen und ihre Grenzen* in 1929. Frankfurt is a central stage in Morgenthau's intellectual development as, through his work for the famous labor lawyer and former social-democratic member of the Weimar National Assembly, Hugo Sinzheimer, Morgenthau became acquainted with some of the most important intellectuals of his time. In Sinzheimer's law office he not only came to know other young scholars, such as Franz Neumann and Ernst Fraenkel, who also worked there as clerks, but he also corresponded with members of the Frankfurt School, such as Theodor W. Adorno, Max Horkheimer and Erich Fromm, as well as with Mannheim. This preoccupation with the Frankfurt School and particularly with the rising struggles of communism and fascism in a declining Weimar Republic fortified Morgenthau's anti-ideological outlook.

1931–33: Acting president of the Frankfurt labor law court

Little is known about Morgenthau's time at the labor law court in Frankfurt. It seems, however, that Morgenthau had realized early on that the personal and professional situation for Jews in Germany was deteriorating, and he left Germany as early as 1932 for Geneva. In accordance with the Law for the Restoration of the Professional Civil Service from April 7, 1933, Morgenthau was officially dismissed from this post on July 11, 1933.

1932–35: *Habilitation* at the Institut des Hautes Études Internationales in Geneva

Morgenthau left Germany for Geneva because he could pursue his postdoctoral thesis (*Habilitation*) there. However, he quickly realized that anti-Semitism does not stop at borders. German professors attacked him personally during his inaugural lecture, and his lectures were largely neglected by students. He also experienced academic misbehavior as his *Habilitation* was torpedoed on personal grounds by his colleague Paul Guggenheim. The thesis, which was published as *"La réalité des normes. En particulier des normes du droit international. Fondement d'une théorie des normes"* in 1934, was only accepted after a positive review by Hans Kelsen, who had arrived shortly before in Geneva. Kelsen was particularly apt to judge Morgenthau's work which dealt extensively with Kelsen's legal positivism. Previously, Morgenthau had published a book devoted to the concept of the political. *La notion du "politique" et la théorie des différends internationaux* from 1933, the translation of which is here published, is to be considered one of his most important contributions to political theory.

1935–36: Faculty position at the Instituto de Estudios Internacionales y Económicos in Madrid

In 1935, the year Morgenthau married Irma Thormann whom he had known since his studies in Munich, he went to Madrid to take up a faculty position like many other German scholars, including Hermann Heller. This time, which he considered to be among the most blissful of his life, came to an abrupt halt when Franco's troops seized Madrid during Morgenthau's honeymoon in Italy.

1937: Emigration to the United States

As Morgenthau was unable to return to Madrid, he and his wife were forced into the precarious life of the refugee, and a veritable odyssey through Europe began before they were able to board the steamship SS *Königstein* in Antwerp on July 17, 1937. His mentor, Hugo Sinzheimer, and old friends from Frankfurt, Richard and Traute Mainzer, saw Morgenthau and his wife off.

1937–39: Faculty position at the Brooklyn College, New York

After starting off as an elevator boy, Morgenthau got his first academic position in the United States at the newly established Brooklyn College (now part of City University). Acquiring an academic position was difficult for him as his only American academic acquaintance who could have spoken in favor of Morgenthau, Richard Gottheil from Columbia University, had died shortly before Morgenthau's arrival. The situation at Brooklyn College was far from ideal as he had to teach numerous subjects on which he was not an expert and which consequently required him to work excessively. Still, it marked the beginning of his exceptional academic career.

1939–43: Assistant professor at the University of Kansas City

The next step was an assistant professorship in law, history, and political science at the University of Kansas City. What seemed to be an intellectual advancement soon turned out to be an impasse. Morgenthau felt alienated as the prevalent style of research and teaching in Kansas City did not match his understanding of scholarship. Still, Kansas City marks an important period in his life. Not only did he become naturalized as an American citizen and admitted to the Missouri bar, his research interests shifted from predominantly legal to almost exclusively political questions. While at the beginning he published in legal journals, during his time in Kansas City he increasingly sought to publish in philosophical and political outlets.

1943–71: Professor at the University of Chicago

Morgenthau reached the apex of his career when he left provincial Kansas City and moved to the University of Chicago in 1943. Originally, he was only supposed to temporarily replace Quincy Wright, but he was offered a permanent position after Wright's return from Washington, and received tenure in 1945. Eventually, he was appointed Albert A. Michelson Distinguished Service Professor of Political Science and Modern History. In Chicago, Morgenthau was at the center of political science as it was the *genius loci* that brought together the different epistemological approaches of American and European émigré scholars. Harold Laswell, Charles Merriam, and Gabriel Almond were important figures that helped to shape the positivistic outlook of the discipline, while Chicago was also the place where the Walgreen Foundation Lectures were held annually, and out of which ground-breaking new thought evolved. Hannah Arendt's *The Human Condition*, Leo Strauss's *Natural Right and History,* and Eric Voegelin's *The New Science of Politics* were delivered there during Morgenthau's years. Also Morgenthau produced some of his most important contributions to political science at that time. In 1946, his first American monograph *Scientific Man vs Power Politics* was published and two years later, in 1948, the first edition of *Politics Among Nations* came out. Since then, it has become one of the best-selling textbooks on International Relations and is now in its seventh edition. In addition, Morgenthau founded the *Center for the Study of American Foreign Policy* (1950–68) and was appointed consultant to the State Department (1949–51) and the Department of Defense (1961–65). At the end of his career in Chicago, Morgenthau became nationally known as one of the first and foremost critics of the Vietnam War.

1968–74: Leonard Davis Distinguished Professor at the City University of New York

After his retirement from Chicago in 1971, Morgenthau moved to New York and became a permanent faculty member at City University. Shortly before, his candidacy for the president of the American Political Science Association had been impeded due to his criticism of American involvement in Indo-China. At City University in 1972, Morgenthau also published his last major monograph: *Science: Servant or Master?*

1974–80: Professor at the New School for Social Research, New York

The final step in his career brought Morgenthau to an institution that had been the haven for many European émigré scholars in their flight from Nazism: the New School for Social Research, also known as the "University in Exile". At one point or another, people like Erich Fromm, Alfred Schütz, Hannah Arendt, Hans Jonas, Leo Strauss, Arnold Brecht, and Emil Lederer – to name only the most well-known social scientists – taught there. During his time at the New School in 1975 Morgenthau was awarded the "Große Bundesverdienstkreuz" (grand Cross of the Order of Merit of the Federal Republic of Germany), one of the highest German civil orders. In 1979, Morgenthau was on his way to China when his plane crashed during an attempt to make a stop-over in Athens. Despite his survival, the long-term consequences of the crash in combination with his overall fragile health, due to tuberculosis in his youth, caused his death on July 19, 1980.

Name Index

Adorno, Theodor W. 6, 24, 26, 71, 155
Alexander the Great 51
Almond, Gabriel 157
Arendt, Hannah 8, 10, 12, 13, 22, 24, 25, 27, 29, 57, 62, 63, 66, 71, 72, 77, 80, 153, 157, 158
Aristophanes 26
Aristotle/Aristotelian 27, 64, 67–9, 71, 75, 77, 140, 153
Ashley, Richard 29, 30, 71

Benjamin, Walter 57, 72
Bismarck, Otto von 12
Brecht, Arnold 158
Burckhardt, Jacob 155
Burckhardt, Walther 16, 137, 142

Castberg, Johan 89, 137, 142
Clausewitz, Carl von 119, 140, 143, 145
Croce, Benedetto 106, 140

Descartes, René 33, 67, 72
Dilthey, Wilhelm 37

Edkins, Jenny 25, 28, 29, 72

Fraenkel, Ernst 6, 155
Fredrick the Great 12
Frei, Christoph 4, 6, 9, 16, 17, 50, 56, 61, 62, 68, 72, 73
Freud, Sigmund 49, 51, 55, 73, 78
Fromm, Erich 6, 49, 155, 158

Giddens, Anthony 54, 67, 73
Goethe, Johann Wolfgang von 10, 79
Gottheil, Richard 10, 156
Guggenheim, Paul 16, 138, 141, 142, 156

Gurian, Waldemar 7

Hegel, Georg Wilhelm Friedrich 20, 65, 140
Heller, Hermann 141, 143, 156
Hindenburg, Paul von 12
Hirst, Paul 28, 29, 73
Hitler, Adolf 12, 23
Homer 26, 117, 143
Horkheimer, Max 6, 24, 26, 71, 155
Huber, Max 105, 137, 139, 143

Jellinek, Georg 16, 28, 155
Johnson, Lyndon B. 15, 151
Jonas, Hans 158

Kelsen, Hans 16–18, 22, 23, 150, 155, 156
Kindermann, Karl Gottfried 3, 23, 40, 45, 73, 76
Kissinger, Henry 3, 39, 40, 69, 73, 76
Kroner, Richard 106, 143

Laswell, Harold 157
Lauterpacht, Hersch 103, 135, 137–39, 143
Lebow, Richard Ned 6, 26, 48, 74
Lederer, Emil 158
Lévinas, Emmanuel 68, 74
Logoz, Paul 16

Mainzer, Richard 156
Mainzer, Traute 156
Mannheim, Karl 6–8, 37, 44, 45, 68, 71, 74, 155
Marcuse, Herbert 6, 24, 25, 27, 74
Marshall-Brown 104, 137, 139, 140, 143, 153
Merriam, Charles 157

Montesquieu, Charles de 140
Mulder, B. 92, 137, 138

Napoleon Bonaparte 51, 70
Neumann, Franz 6, 10, 155
Neumeyer Herbert, Rita 10, 75
Neumeyer, Karl 13, 54
Nietzsche, Friedrich 35, 37, 43, 57–62, 68, 77, 79, 155

Oakeshott, Michael 48, 56, 57, 75
Oncken, Hermann 6, 154

Plessner, Helmuth 53, 106, 144

Rickert, Heinrich 43

Schmitt, Carl 7, 16, 18–23, 45, 60, 68, 73, 74, 78, 106, 108, 109, 112, 118, 139–41, 144–46, 155
Schopenhauer, Arthur 62, 79
Schütz, Alfred 8, 9, 11, 37, 68, 78, 79, 158
Simmel, Georg 8, 9, 37, 62, 79, 155

Sinzheimer, Hugo 6, 7, 10, 11, 49, 79, 141, 144, 155, 156
Smend, Rudolph 19, 106, 139, 141, 144
Strauss, Leo 140, 145, 157, 158
Strisower, Leo 89, 137, 141, 145

Thormann, Irma 156

Verzijl, J. H. W 92, 137, 138, 145
Voegelin, Eric 6, 157

Walker, R. B. J. 29, 30, 71
Weber, Cynthia 31
Weber, Max 6, 43, 54–6, 63, 68–71, 74, 78, 79, 141, 145, 155
Wehberg, Hans 104, 138–40, 144, 145
Wight, Martin 50
Williams, Michael C. 3, 18, 47, 80
Wölfflin, Heinrich 6, 155
Wright, Quincy 157

Young-Bruehl, Elisabeth 10, 57, 62, 80

Subject Index

a priori 21, 33, 38, 65
alienation 8–11, 154–55
American Political Science
    Association 14, 158
"animal laborans" 27, 61
arbitration 88, 94, 98, 138, 140

bureaucratization 23, 24, 27
capitalism/capitalist 24, 25, 27

China 13, 115, 149, 150, 151,
    152, 158
Cobourg (Germany) 6, 9, 154
common good 27, 52, 62, 63, 64
conditionality/conditionalities 7, 44
Conservatism/conservative 7,
    53, 148
constructivism/constructivist 37
Covenant of the League of
    Nations 94, 136, 137, 141
Critical Theory 24–30, 66

*"Der Selbstmord mit gutem
    Gewissen"(Suicide with good
    conscious)* 26, 65, 69, 74, 146
*Derivation of the political from the
    nature of man* 20, 141
*"Die internationale Rechtspflege,
    ihr Wesen und ihre Grenzen"
    (International Judicature, its
    nature and limits)* 4, 74, 85,
    137, 138, 146
diplomacy 22, 28, 39, 74,
    127, 147, 152
disenchantment of the world 6,
    30, 77
dispute(s) 15, 22, 29, 81, 83, 84–141
  concept of 95
    international 81, 85, 87, 88, 103,
      105, 108, 125, 126, 128, 129,
      135, 138

legal 88–95, 137, 138
  legal merit of 104
  objective nature of 91
  political 22, 85, 86, 87, 97, 99,
    100, 103, 104, 121, 135
  pure 95, 129, 132
dissent/dissidence 6, 11, 30, 32,
    60, 71, 79
"domaine réservé" 97, 136

émigré scholar 10, 157, 158
empiricism/empiricist 33–7, 42,
    67, 68, 78
Enlightenment 26, 52
"Erfahrungswissenschaft" 34
ethics 27, 45, 63, 67, 68, 70, 71, 72,
    74, 75, 147
European Coal and Steel
    Community 5

fascism 7, 26, 53, 54, 56, 155
foreign policy 22, 35, 39, 44,
    73, 75, 77, 96, 118, 132,
    147, 148, 149, 150, 151, 152,
    153, 157
Frankfurt School 7, 155
'friend' and 'foe' 19, 22, 60,
    108, 111–18

Geneva 5, 15, 16, 17, 22, 148,
    155, 156
German Empire 7, 53
Germany 5, 6, 10, 23, 24, 48,
    54, 148, 154, 155, 158
Greece 97

Hague Convention 89, 137
Holocaust 11, 25, 55
hubris 26, 27, 45, 67
human condition 25–7, 38,
    67, 71, 157

human nature 20, 38, 42, 49, 51,
    56, 65, 69
humanities 5, 15, 16, 23, 24, 36,
    37, 63
humanity 22, 25, 27, 28
humanization 23, 24

idealism/idealist 26, 33–9, 42,
    67, 68
ideology/ideologies/ideological 6, 7,
    12, 23, 24, 26, 28, 29, 39, 53,
    54, 56, 57, 58, 60, 61, 71, 72,
    74, 152, 153
  anti-ideological 6, 10, 155
  ideologization 16, 17, 54, 57, 58
imperialism (of categories) 65, 72,
    73, 144
Institute for Social Research
    (Frankfurt) 6, 49
Institute of International Law
    104, 140
interest 3, 4, 8, 13, 14, 16, 18, 20,
    23, 25, 35, 36, 38, 39, 40, 43,
    44, 47, 48, 50–2, 54, 56, 57,
    60, 63, 64, 66, 68, 69, 73, 74,
    75, 77, 78, 88, 89, 91, 95, 97,
    98, 99, 100, 104, 118, 123,
    129, 134, 148, 154, 157
  national interest 39, 40, 69, 73,
    75, 77, 148
international law 4, 74, 75, 87,
    88–90, 92–5, 97, 100, 104,
    105, 121, 124–28, 135, 136,
    139, 140, 141, 147, 148
International Relations (the
    discipline of) 3, 4, 5, 15, 22,
    24, 28, 29, 30, 31, 35, 36, 37,
    38, 44, 45, 46, 47, 48, 56, 60,
    62, 72–80, 96, 102, 105, 108,
    127, 149, 150–52, 157
  intellectual history of 4, 37,
    42, 69

Japan 97, 152
Jurisprudence 4
"jus pacis" 105

justice/injustice 22, 58, 63,
    87, 94, 104, 126, 127, 137,
    138, 144, 152

knowledge 5, 9, 31, 33, 34, 35, 36,
    43, 44, 45, 46, 51, 53, 54, 59,
    65, 67, 70, 73
  conditionality of/contingency
    of 7, 8, 23, 31, 68
  sociology of 3, 37, 44
Korea 5
"Kraft" 47, 69

"*La Réalité des Normes. En
    particulier des normes du droit
    international. Fondement d'une
    théorie des normes*" (*The reality
    of norms in international law.
    On the foundations of a theory
    or norms*) 4, 55, 75, 146
law of nations 89, 90, 142
League of Nations 5, 94, 136, 137,
    141
"l'esprit des lois" 140
liberalism 7, 10, 23, 53, 150

"Macht" 47, 48, 76, 77, 144, 150, 152
Marxism 7
metaphysics/metaphysical 6, 16, 20,
    52, 59, 62, 108, 118, 148
modernity 16, 24–8, 78
morality 19, 21, 35, 38, 39, 40, 62,
    73, 107–12, 147

National Socialism/national
    socialist 12, 24, 25
norm, normative 4, 5, 6, 8, 18, 19,
    20, 22, 23, 25, 27, 47, 48, 52,
    55, 57, 62, 63, 67, 69, 70, 72,
    75, 85, 88, 89, 90, 92, 93, 95,
    121, 122, 123, 124, 126, 127,
    130, 135, 137, 146, 156
NSDAP 9, 154
nuclear armament 5

objectification 21, 29, 121

objectivity 6, 11, 21, 42–4, 65, 67, 69, 70

"pacta sunt servanda" 89
Pan-American Conference, Second (1902) 99
Pariah 6, 8, 30, 71
peace 22, 23, 25, 39, 69, 77, 79, 87, 98, 100, 106, 123, 124, 131, 140, 142, 147, 150, 151, 153
Peace Conference in The Hague, First (1899) 89, 98, 137
Peace Conference in The Hague, Second (1907) 89, 98, 100, 137
Permanent Court of International Justice 94, 104, 137
perspectivist 7, 44
political religion 6
political science 4, 6, 11, 14, 22, 34, 36, 42, 45, 75, 76, 79, 147, 148, 157, 158
re-politicization 23–5, 27
de-politicization 28–9, 52, 60
Politics among Nations 3, 13, 40, 55, 56, 57, 77, 153, 157
Politics in the Twentieth Century 4, 76, 150
positivism/positivist 7, 12, 17, 18, 22–5, 28, 32, 34–7, 41–3, 45, 66, 75, 90, 103, 106, 140, 147, 156, 157
post-structuralism/post-structuralist 24–5, 28, 29–32, 66
power 4, 5, 6, 10, 11, 14, 15, 17, 18, 20, 23, 25, 27, 29, 30, 35, 36, 38, 39, 40–4, 45, 47–64
antagonism of interests 23, 29, 42, 57, 64
force 14, 15, 34, 41, 42, 58, 59, 60, 69, 83, 86, 106, 108, 119, 123, 124–29, 132–33, 151
love 19, 41, 42, 49–51, 57, 61, 69, 76, 80, 150

"amor fati" 57, 58
"amor mundi" 57, 64
"pouvoir" 47, 49, 52, 57, 83, 86, 122–25
"puissance" 42, 47, 49, 52, 56–7, 59–62, 67, 70, 83, 118, 122–25, 131
spheres of 86, 121–22, 124–25, 128
twofold concept of 5, 20, 47–64, 66, 67, 70
public law 16, 18, 87, 105, 136
public sphere 12, 13, 22, 23, 24, 25, 66

rationalism/rationalist 33, 35–7, 41–2, 45, 48, 67, 68, 78
'realism as revolt against historical optimism' 23
"rebus sic stantibus" 134
reification 21, 45, 54, 65
Russia 98

Science: Servant or Master? 4, 5, 51, 52, 59, 61, 62, 77, 152, 158
Scientific Man vs. Power Politics 4, 10, 11, 45, 48, 68, 75, 78, 147, 157
scientification 23, 24, 36
scientism 7, 23, 36, 48
"Six Principles of Political Realism" 3, 35, 36, 38, 42–4, 46, 68, 77, 140
social engineering 24, 45
social planning 23, 24, 28, 41, 66, 68, 75, 147
social science 5, 15, 16, 23, 24, 36, 37, 63, 68, 73, 78, 147, 149
Socialism/socialist 7, 53
sociology of knowledge 3, 31, 44
sovereignty 7, 28, 29, 30, 53, 93, 136, 147
Spain 5, 10
"spheres of elasticity" 22, 23
"Staatslehre"/"Staatsrechtslehre" 7, 15, 16, 17, 19, 22, 23, 65, 74, 139, 144, 146, 156

"Standortgebundenheit"/
     "standortgebunden" 8,
     43–6, 67, 68
student protests 13
Switzerland 5, 10, 98, 147

technologization 28
tension 79, 83, 128–33, 135, 149
The Purpose of American Politics 11,
     59, 149, 150
Third Reich 7
totalitarianism/totalitarian 12–14,
     24, 25, 27, 74, 153
Treaty of Arbitration between Brazil
     and Chile (1899) 138
Truth and Power 4, 17, 77, 152

*"Über den Sinn der Wissenschaft
     in dieser Zeit und über die
     Bestimmung des Menschen"*
     (*On the meaning of humanities
     and the nature of men*) 5, 52,
     75, 146
"Übermensch" 58–60
United Nations 5, 147, 148, 149, 151
University of Chicago 27, 62, 66,
     68, 69, 157
University of Frankfurt 6
University of Munich 6, 23

Vietnam/Vietnam War 5, 13, 48
violence 27, 44, 55, 62, 63, 69, 71,
     122–23

weapons of mass destruction 5, 60
Weimar Republic 5, 6, 7, 12,
     16, 22, 155
world community 5
world view 3–9, 11, 12, 13, 15, 26,
     30, 54, 65, 67

"zoon politikon" 40